Things a *Woman* Should Know *About Shoes*

Things a
Woman
Should Know
About Shoes

Karen Homer

PRION

First published in Great Britain in 2008 by

Prion
an imprint of the
Carlton Publishing Group
20 Mortimer Street
London W1T 3JW

10 9 8 7 6 5 4 3 2 1

Text copyright © Karen Homer 2008
Design copyright © Carlton Publishing Group 2008

The right of Karen Homer to be identified as the author of this work
has been asserted by her in accordance with the Copyright, Designs
and Patents Act 1988

ISBN 978-1-85375-635-1

Printed and bound in Singapore

Contents

Introduction

'Give a girl the right shoes and she can conquer the world!'
Bette Midler

Women love shoes. Even women who couldn't care less about fashion can appreciate the line of a finely turned heel. Small girls (and in my experience small boys too) covet their mother's evening shoes and will totter precariously, and surprisingly confidently, as soon as they learn to walk. Women who have lifestyles that demand nothing but 'sensible shoes' or no cash to spare have closets full of designer stilettos unworn in their boxes. Others, slovenly in all matters to do with housekeeping, meticulously dust and polish a favourite pair of shoes. The worst offenders pretend not to care and chuck thousands of pounds' worth of cobbling into the dark recesses of their understairs cupboard – a telling-off for you later.

Women have as many fetishes about shoes as men do. For every woman who is obsessed with stilettos as her only means to glamour there is one whose lust is for boots – riding, walking, motorbiking – despite spending most of her time in the car. For another the siren call comes from a particular brand of sandal – one in every colour. Or the irresistible allure of satin mules, fluffy slippers, studded-sole 'driving shoes', you name it, there is some woman out there with a serious habit. And those who scoff at the notion of having a 'shoe thing' please count the number of pairs of trainers you own. You're as bad as the others then!

This is a book for all women – and let's not forget men – for whom the mere thought of new shoes prompts an involuntary sigh of pleasure. Better than sex? Maybe. Of course the two are intrinsically linked or so the advertising men would have us believe. Can the right shoes get you your man? A new job? Change your personality? Certainly shoes can change the way you feel about yourself by simply changing the way you walk. And changing your shoes is the simplest way to transform your outfit.

The following chapters are devoted to shoes of all kinds, full of advice on making your habit work for you, tips on downsizing your collection or picking new essentials. There are consoling stories of those who have the bug much worse than you do and horror stories that we can all relate to. If your feet are suffering from an overdose of too-small pointy shoes, find some remedies or simply buy a bigger pair. And if you discover that it *isn't* true that your feet don't get fat, don't despair, shoes can be stretched – a little at least.

So slip into your best stillies, mules or Uggs, preferably while still wearing pyjamas, and read on.

One Step at a Time
– a brief history of shoes

150 years ago things started looking up for the shoe-lover.

The rise of American manufacturing and the invention of the practical, flexible sole in 1860 kick-started the mass production of footwear, allowing the United States to rival Paris in the shoe industry. And the cost-cutting this allowed opened up the possibility of owning more than one pair! But what was the point of buying more than one pair if they were all the same?

And so it all began. Shoes were designed for different occasions, heels were made from both leather and wood, and along

Things a Woman Should Know About Shoes

Shoes have been around a lot longer than credit cards, and although the very first shoes would have been purely practical – made from animal skins that eventually underwent tanning to preserve them and make them stronger – it was not long before shoes became equated with status and fashion. In the Ancient World of Greece, Rome and Egypt the wearing of shoes or sandals was the norm, and only the very poor, or those like Socrates who shunned shoes for ascetic reasons, went without. (And as Plato notes in his Symposium, even the famous philosopher would bathe and put on some shoes for a drinking party.)

Although sandals were not particularly ostentatious in the Ancient World, decorative discs and gilded straps were not uncommon and there was a clear distinction between men's and women's shoes. There was certainly an erotic element to the shoe as depicted in vase-painting and sculpture from the time – Aphrodite withholding a shoe from Pan, Eros fluttering overhead – and the practice of matrimonial shoe-lacing whereby a new bride's special wedding shoes were symbolically tied.

By the time we reach medieval Italy shoes have diversified to include sandals, boots, clogs, slippers and more. Peasants wore clogs made of wood or cork, while members of the Italian courts preferred a delicate velvet or silk shoe. It even became necessary to pass legislation to prevent excessive height or a particular kind of fabric being used in shoe-making, mainly of the pianelle: instantly recognizable shoes with an inches-high bridge or platform heel. These had erotic appeal in the way they affected a woman's gait and yet their lack of easy mobility was not dissimilar to that of the Chinese practice of foot-binding.

Even more excessive was the Venetian chopine, a staggeringly high-heeled platform – recorded as high as 24 inches – worn in Europe between the fourteenth and seventeenth centuries. Here fashion firmly took hold, with contemporaries being able to decipher a person's social status from the thickness of sole. The high cost and extravagant adornment of the chopine, all to flaunt status, led to further legislation and intervention from both Church and State. The association between the chopine and the courtesan is well remarked upon by commentators and artists alike.

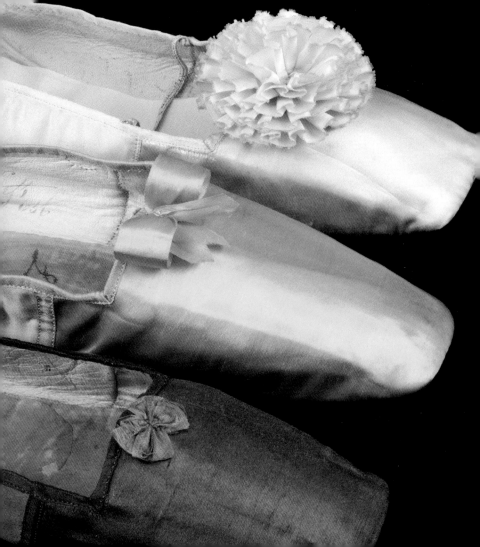

The eighteenth century saw a marked change in shoes, As keeping above the filth of street level became less important thanks to the improvement of public spaces. The French popularized smaller and more delicate shoes, and Paris began to be known as the fashion capital of Europe. Around this time, men bade farewell to seventeenth-century ornate footwear: men's shoes became restrained, not unlike those of today, whereas women's began a flight of fancy. Satin, silk and brocade were common fabrics, elaborate buckles of silver, gold or bronze were the jewellery of the foot, and the silk stocking completed the look. Buckles also allowed the wearer to customize a shoe for any occasion.

By the beginning of the nineteenth century French fashion had taken a firm hold, usurping the red heels and buckles of courtly shoes. Simpler forms with a narrow, lengthy shape, a black or white exterior, pale inside and a square toe, eventually sporting a rosette, were not unlike the ubiquitous ballet pumps with their little tied bows that are so fashionable today. This was also a time when the health of the foot and the consequences of deformity from ill-fitting shoes began to be acknowledged.

Last but not least was the Victorian influence, extending to the black 'Balmoral' boot. Along with this came a taste for more modest footwear, lest anyone be tempted by a stray erotic flash of a finely turned ankle.

with black and white kid-leather uppers, consumers might now choose suede and reptile skins in a variety of colours. Shoes were officially a fashion item, with those deemed less fashionable being worn by the working classes as new styles came into vogue.

If you have ever deliberated over which shoes to put with which outfit or wondered if you can get away with the same pair at work, in the office and out on the town, consider the etiquette challenges of your early-twentieth-century sister: boudoir slippers in the morning, low shoes with fastenings in the afternoon, kid or satin slippers in the evening; outdoor boots should be plain for walking, more ornate for visiting or carriage trips – it adds a whole new dimension to the concept of taxi-shoe. This was all before even considering riding boots, tennis shoes, canvas shoes for boating, etc. An expensive habit for a well-dressed lady.

Things a Woman Should Know About Shoes

The woman on the street, however, usually made do with two or three pairs – and the rigid rules as to which shoe should be worn with what outfit began to be challenged as a less-well-off but sartorially aware woman might be unable to resist a pair of beautifully delicate satin slippers and find herself (shock, horror!) having to wear them on the street as well as indoors. Well, why not?

And so, by giving women options to choose from, shoe-manufacturers gave them the freedom to express themselves a little more. Early-twentieth-century suffragettes wore heels to establish their femininity. The 1920s flapper flaunted her legs in high heels and short skirts – the original dancing shoes. More importantly, this is when shoes became sexy.

Things a Woman Should Know About Shoes

Platforms versus heels?

'I don't know who invented the high heel but all women owe him a lot.'

Marilyn Monroe

The high heels of the 1920s and '30s libertarian were more kittenish than stiletto-vamp (we are still a few decades off the invention of the spike-heel) but they were still the sexiest option. Platforms, on the other hand, popularized in the 1930s and '40s by high-profile designers such as Salvatore Ferragamo, had made the transformation from beach-wear to high-fashion, yet to the woman (or man) on the street they still didn't have that erotic appeal.

Finally, by the mid-1950s the stiletto arrived! Teetering legs, swaying hips, breasts thrust forward – need I say more? Whatever you think about the stiletto it must be doing something right because there is no doubt it is here to stay.

By the 1960s the counter-culture that was women's liberation and the burgeoning hippy movement wasn't just saying burn your bra but chuck out your heels. Along with the fashion for mini-dresses, Twiggy-style gamine-look flat shoes seemed to be making a comeback. And neat block heels à la Jackie Kennedy somehow seemed chicer, not to mention easier to walk in.

But there was hope for the platform yet, in the shape of 1970s disco fever and the staggeringly high glitter platforms that graced the feet of not only female but also male glam-rock stars. Clunky, wedgy, generally unflattering to the foot – you might think that the 1970s, with all its other style crimes, would have dispatched these heels to history. But unfortunately not. There is currently a worrying renaissance of platforms by the high-fashion houses if not on the street – which just goes to show that fashion really does recycle itself.

The 1980s needed a suitably menacing heel to match the killer shoulder pads, so back came the stiletto, dominatrix-style this time. And so it went on, with the cult of *Sex and the City* and the ubiquitous presence of Jimmy Choo on the red carpet. The flip-side of fashionable footwear is, of course, the cult of the training shoe, but more about that later.

So there you have it – the rise and fall of the shoe. Is it any wonder we are all so addicted?

Perfect Pins

'It is the flagrant lack of practicality that makes high-heeled shoes so fascinating.'

Stephen Bayley

So, you've accepted that stilettos are an essential part of any fashionable woman's wardrobe. You venture into a shoe shop – a boutique even, if your bank balance allows it. You spot a luscious pair of not-too-high (or so you think), delicately formed, pointed-at-the-toe, gently moulded round the heel, black satin shoes. Just the kind of shoe staple that every woman should have to match little black dresses, mannish tuxedoes or even a business suit when a promotion is due.

We have the Italians to thank for the perfection of the stiletto heel when they discovered that by inserting a metal spike through the length of the heel it would support the wearer's weight – despite the area base being that of a drawing pin. Sound painful? It is.

The 1950s were the decade when the stiletto was truly the only heel to be seen in. Hollywood divas like Marilyn Monroe may have set the trend but even the housewife at the kitchen stove felt duty bound to wear a pair – perfect kitsch in her tight-waisted, full-skirted frock, a delicate apron tied round her middle.

But it didn't end there. Since the 1980s stilettos have grown and grown, with heels as high as seven inches and designs that might be classified as lethal weapons. Manolo Blahnik's metal-spike heel, for example, could take out an intruder with ease – eventually he was forced to withdraw it from sale as it was accused of being a lethal weapon. It is no wonder that when they were first invented stilettos were banned from certain areas lest they damage the floor. Anyone with stylish stripped-wooden floors will agree.

Things a Woman Should Know About Shoes

You call over the assistant; she *isn't* wearing stilettos, you notice, but then on your feet all day, who would be? Your size is a six, or in this shop a Continental European 39. The pair is lifted from its tissue-lined box, more a work of art than an item of footwear – this is the fantasy. You poise your foot to enter the shoe and hold your breath.

But something is wrong. The foot that looked so lovely after you gave yourself a pedicure is looking ugly: swollen, red and angry, and distinctly fatter than your chosen shoe. Determined, you press on, but your toes barely squeeze into the fronts and there is no way your heels are going in at the same time. Not quite the Cinderella-slipping-into-her-glass-slipper experience you had hoped for.

Lesson one: teeny-tiny pointed shoes often need to be bought one, if not two, sizes bigger. And even if you manage to squeeze yourself into a too-small pair you will soon regret it as your cramped feet force the leather outwards, giving that unattractive bulging effect.

Lesson two: the typically elegant stiletto with its elongated shape and pointed toe is never that comfortable. This is a sacrifice you have to make.

Lesson three: stock up with plasters, blister cream and foot balm – but NEVER, as if this needs to be spelled out, allow any kind of dressing to poke out of the shoe itself. If you do you might as well not be wearing them.

To make you feel better: I saw a picture not that long ago of Victoria Beckham in the back of a limousine on her way home from some event having kicked off her trademark killer heels. I grant it may have been an unkind angle, but her feet looked positively misshapen. Nothing a good pedi or trip to the podiatrist wouldn't help with, I'm sure, but it made me realize the sacrifice these celebrities make for their image.

Lesson four: look after your feet. You may want to torture them to look good on occasion but make it up to them afterwards. More on that later in the book.

When you do find a pair you can squeeze into, and stand up (mental note, don't go shoe-shopping wearing baggy old jeans more suited to trainers. You will have to roll them up, and a fine shoe on the end of an unshaven, winter-white leg detracts from the glamour somewhat), something strange has happened to your centre of gravity.

This is a fact, not an illusion.

Things a Woman Should Know About Shoes

High-heeled shoes, and stilettos in particular, totally change the way you stand. Your centre of gravity is thrust forward, forcing a sway in your back and sending your bosom sailing forth like Queen Victoria's.

The first thing to do when you step into a pair of heels is to adjust your posture. If you can, try tipping your weight back onto the heel of the shoe. The worst high-heel agony comes from balancing on the ball of your foot. In fact, angling your weight backwards is how we all should be walking anyway (Masai warrior style, see MBTs later!) so this is good advice for all shoe-wearing. It may feel strange at first, but I promise you won't fall over backwards and you'll be doing your back a favour.

Now take a step.

A bit like learning to walk all over again, I know, but soon you'll be more confident. Once you have relaxed, enjoy the reason women – and, ok, men – love stilettos so much. Your hips start to sway, your legs go on forever, you feel sassy, confident, sexy – not like you at all.

Welcome to our world.

A few more things to bear in mind:

The highest heel a woman can walk in sensibly is five and a half inches. The six-inch heel is a myth. Shoe fetishists might disagree, but consider – how much walking do you do in those kinky boots anyway?

Couture-made four-inch heels are as easy to walk in as a pair of trainers. Well, almost. It is more about the shape of the shoe than its height, and if something is tailored *exactly* to the shape of your foot it will ease pressure, aid balance and make you feel as if you are dancing on air. Ok, the champagne does that, not the shoes, but you know what I mean.

If you really, *really* can't learn to walk in stilettos, opt for heels that are wide at the top and taper down to a half-inch square at the bottom. The effect is similar and certainly better than falling over like an idiot.

And last but not least ... there are heels other than stilettos.

There are many heel shapes that don't strictly conform to the stiletto but are just as sexy, just as feminine, often very high fashion and best of all, more comfortable!

Manolo Blahnik praises the kitten heel, also known as the Sabrina heel, a narrow but low heel popularized by Audrey Hepburn in the movie of that name. It is one of those shapes that is sometimes high fashion, other times simply a staple of the stylish woman's wardrobe.

High-heeled pumps tend to have a much wider – though still high – heel and are certainly more suitable for the office than a stiletto if you do want height. The smaller versions of these can either look retro and chic 1950s or frumpy in a matching-handbag-and-concrete-Harrods-helmet-hairstyle kind of way. Be careful.

For stiletto sceptics there are plenty of memorable heels – for example those by Roger Vivier, the iconic shoe designer, who has several instantly recognizable and eminently stylish shapes that he regularly uses.

Cinderella Complex
– sex and the shoe

'It's really hard to walk in a single woman's shoes — that's why you sometimes need really special shoes!'
Sarah Jessica Parker as Carrie Bradshaw in *Sex and the City*

Now that you've mastered the art of the stiletto it would seem churlish not to point out its added benefit.

The right shoe will get you your man. Not necessarily the right man, granted, but certainly *a* man, if that is what you are after.

Bear in mind that in certain circles there is a sense that 'nice girls don't wear stilettos'.

Shoe fetishism can be traced back to the eighteenth century with the enormous height of the Venetian chopine. Historians suggest that the difficulty in walking in these shoes, in common with their spike-heeled contemporary counterparts, can be seen as a form of erotic bondage. It was at this time, too, that men stopped wearing heels and the latter became firmly associated with women.

Fetishists have always revered the high heel, often pushing the boundaries of height far further than fashion. Combined with the corset, early-twentieth-century shoe 'kinkiness' was here to stay. A correspondent to *London Life* in 1913 wrote that 'the love of high heels is one of our kinks . . . and a harmless one at that.'

For the most extreme examples we only have to look to shoe museums around the world to see late-nineteenth-century fetishists' impossibly high heels that might even have been designed with a more explicit sexual purpose. And in pornography there are descriptions of stabbing, scratching and penetration from the heel.

There are plenty of ways to attribute eroticism to shoes, from the image of the humiliated man kissing a woman's feet to the dominatrix who presses her heels to the throat of her prone victim. Consider the sexual connotations of contemporary usage of the term 'toe cleavage' to describe the bulging over the front of an open toe. Or the suggestion that if parts of the foot equate to parts of the body, what does the revealed heel of a slingback suggest? No wonder Frederick's of Hollywood named one shoe 'Open 'n' Inviting'. And it is no surprise that some of the most extreme erotic shoes – staggering high heels in black patent leather, for example – are made in large sizes for transvestites.

Boots, too have sexual connotations. Picture the classic stereotype of the prostitute in thigh-high heeled boots. Or the corset-like lacing that some thigh-high boots are decorated with.

It seems that shoe fetishism is as alive and well today as ever before.

Things a Woman Should Know About Shoes

Luckily the stiletto heel doesn't have an absolute monopoly on the sexy shoe market. Anything delicate and narrow will do the trick, although perhaps not as dramatically as sitting in a bar suggestively dangling a pair of f***-off high heels. One way to get a free drink.

'There is no unhappier creature on earth that a fetishist who yearns to embrace a woman's shoe and had to embrace the whole woman.'

Karl Kraus

So why are shoes sexy?

There are several theories:

The shoe is a phallic symbol, which makes it as an object intrinsically sexy. Hmm, this might work for some seriously kinky buttoned-up conservatives, but for your average girl on the street it is not convincing.

It is what the shoe does to the *foot* that makes it sexy. This is more likely. The theory is that tight-fitting high heels are a form of bondage – a bit like a corset – and there *is* a certain frisson

of pretty red ballerina pumps, worn with white Capri pants and a navy-and-white striped top, are simply St Tropez chic, and demure with it.

A pair of red sandals, delicately strapped and flat heeled, are a perfect match for pillar-box-red toes in summer.

Everything comes in red these days – trainers, Birkenstocks, fluffy bedroom slippers, none of which spell S-E-X too clearly. Personally I would say a pair of plain Christian Louboutin high-heeled black pumps with their trademark flash of scarlet heel are a lot sexier than an overt attempt at wearing sexy red shoes.

The moral of the story, and worth remembering where all shoes are concerned, is that shoes are only part of an outfit. If your dress is skimpy, your heels are high and red is part of the package, the overall effect spells danger.

I am a big fan of red shoes, but of the chic, demure variety that means summer fun and playfulness. Remember, pillar-box red is one of the most classic colours of all, and mixed with black, navy or white it is about as safe as you can get.

Designer Made

Shoes are one of the most important consumer items in the world of high-end designer fashion.

Relatively speaking, shoes are at the cheaper end of the scale of designer purchases you might make.

Cheap*er*, you understand, not cheap. A pair of off-the-peg designer shoes will set you back upwards of £300. And that includes the sandals that are a mere wisp of pearlized leather.

Venture into the serious couture market and a pair of Jimmy Choos – made by Jimmy Choo Couture, the part of the business retained by the man himself – will start at around £500. These are often made from a pre-designed model but tailored to the measurements of your foot, resulting in exquisite comfort even in the highest heel – I know, I stood for hours at my wedding reception in a pair.

For the really wealthy, Sergio Rossi has launched a service called Foot Couture in which an entire shoe is designed from drawing board upwards, working with the creative director to make the perfect pair of shoes exclusively for you. But this doesn't come cheap – try £1,500 a pair plus!

Before you faint at the thought of spending so much on a pair of shoes, change your mindset. Think about it as an investment. (Women have used this excuse for years, so why stop now?) A pair of stunning shoes make a cheap Top Shop dress look like it comes from Prada. A pair of cheap shoes worn with a Prada dress make it looks as if it comes from Oxfam, especially given Prada's proclivity for unfinished hemlines and rather retro-dowdy frocks. Dress costs £700, shoes cost half that and you can wear them with more than one outfit. You can do the maths.

But you have to pick your designer and your shoes carefully. A real pair of statement shoes – the must-have fashion item of that season – is as noticeable as any other garment with a limited shelf-life.

Things a Woman Should Know About Shoes

Of course it depends on what you want. If quality, longevity and investment are what you want, buy plain – a classic pair of black satin Manolo high-heeled pumps will have you looking like Audrey Hepburn for years to come. But if flamboyant dressing is more your style then get what you pay for and go for creativity, colour and maximum visibility.

Shoes are a way to express your more exotic tastes while retaining a degree of subtlety. Think leopard-print shoe versus leopard-print dress. Rather like a classy A-list actress versus a tacky celebrity housemate.

And even if your purchase does look dated a season later, shoes, unlike clothes, are a work of art – literally, if you do as a friend of mine does and rotate them on the mantel shelf in the bedroom.

But which designer?

A disclaimer: this is by no means a definitive list. Many fashion designers also do shoes, and many shoe designers now branch out into other accessories and even clothes. This is a list of some of the greats, the quirks and the seducers. Useful if dipping a metaphorical toe into the world of upmarket shoes for the first time.

Things a Woman Should Know About Shoes

Jimmy Choo: off-the-peg means classic red-carpet stilettos, St. Tropez jewelled sandals and a certain degree of glitz and glamour, worn by every celebrity, Hollywood actress and jet-setter you can think of. Couture can mean anything you like although the designs in store are typically feminine and stylish. Favoured by the more discreet wealthy and those in public life who need to match outfits – Princess Diana was a regular.

Manolo Blahnik: the only on-the-street name from his launch in London in the early 1970s until Choo was popularized by Tamara Mellon in the 1990s. The godfather of the designer shoe, working without assistants, creates every one of his thousands of designs from sketch to chiselling the last, to moulding and sculpting the heel: a true perfectionist. A wardrobe essential for any serious shoe-lover, Blahniks inspire extreme reactions – as in the case of Carrie Bradshaw in *Sex and the City*, who pleaded with a mugger, 'Just don't take my Manolo Blahniks.'

Roger Vivier: the flamboyant maestro of French shoe design has been credited with the invention of the stiletto in the 1950s and designs that really can be called works of art. The company that bears his name since his death in 1998 is enjoying a renaissance in London since the opening of a fashionable new boutique. Very 'now', his designs are unmistakeable – serious shoe fashionistas only need apply.

Christian Louboutin: another French legend, Louboutin is famous for his trademark red-soled shoes in a palette of delicate pastels and nail-polish brights. Leopard-prints, decorative buckles and flourishes and metallic finishes make his designs stand out. Fundamentally sexy. With that pillar-box flash of sole as you walk, buy these if you want everyone to know where your shoes are from. Has a loyal clientele, including Sarah Jessica Parker and Madonna.

Terry de Havilland: legendary British shoe-maker, a stalwart of the King's Road scene since the 1950s and beloved of the rock 'n' roll set including David and Angie Bowie, Anita Pallenberg and Bianca Jagger. Despite going underground in the 1980s he has re-emerged in the last couple of years for twenty-first-century rock chicks to enjoy.

Salvatore Ferragamo: the Italian legend who even has a shoe museum in Florence named after him. Celebrated designer of Dorothy's ruby slippers in *The Wizard of Oz*, his is a prestigious name in fashion. A clothes as well as an accessories designer, his shoes are not as ostentatious as those of some Italians but beautifully crafted in classic shapes and colours. Perfect for ladies who lunch.

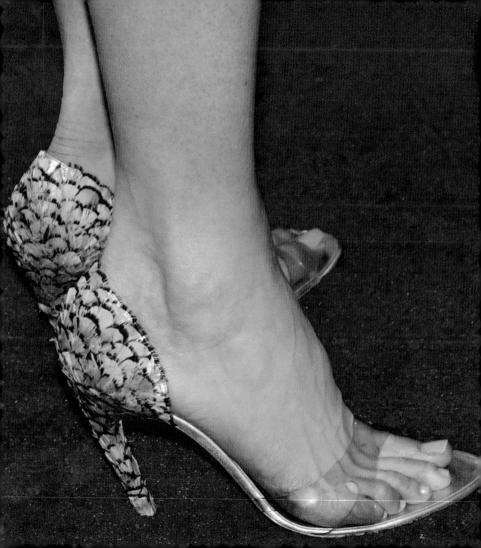

Things a Woman Should Know About Shoes

Sergio Rossi: if colourful and sexy is what you are after, this Italian designer offers up La Dolce Vita wedges, bejewelled sandals and killer patent heels for vamps and seductresses.

Roberto Cavalli: the Italian fashion designer beloved of Victoria Beckham and Kate Moss is primarily a clothes designer but his shoes reflect his love of sexy animal-prints and acid colours with plenty of vibrant linings, gold and glitter. Perfect for party animals.

Robert Clergerie: this Parisien is not as wedded to stilettos as some and has a typically chic collection of block heels and flat sandals, delicately adorned without being over-the-top. Perfect for stylish, classic dressers who like a little flair about their feet.

Charles Jourdan: the French fashion designer born in the same year as Coco Chanel spent many years innovating shoe designs with new fabrics. His label is famous for the basic pump, both flat and stiletto in a rainbow of colours. Perhaps more fashion-forward in the past, he still provides classic shoes and wardrobe staples for women who need to be smartly dressed.

JP Tods: the invention of the now-ubiquitous driving shoe is the responsibility of Tods. These shoes, part of the crisp Ralph Lauren slacks-and-white-shirt uniform of upper-crust

New Yorkers, are also beloved of anyone who values comfort. Available in every colour and now in a variety of seasonal as well as classic designs, they are beautifully soft, exquisitely easy on the feet and much, much copied on the high street.

Patrick Cox: worth a mention to keep up the British contingent among all those French and Italians. His shoes, now that his mid-1990s heyday when we all wore his Wannabes is over, are kind of funky with a little English eccentricity.

Gucci: How can we forget the dreaded logo-loafer with those memorable entwined Gs, symbol of 1980s excess and ostentation? Well, we have, although the designer still favours conspicuous consumption, with logo'd fabric trainers and loafers among more feminine designs. For die-hard label fans only.

Prada: another label that suffers from over-branding but many of the designs are typically quirky and feminine, suiting the design ethos of the clothes. Sports shoes are a massive seller and good, comfortable, not too ostentatious (see above), but expensive for what they are. Paying for the name might not be worth it.

Things a Woman Should Know About Shoes

Stephane Kelian: I've included this Paris designer because I love his shoes. His sculpted designs use trademark woven leather to great effect, particularly the wedge-heeled sandals. Hard to get hold of but worth the effort.

Vivienne Westwood: last but not least, who could forget that famous Naomi Campbell tumble off towering Westwood platforms – did it make or break her reputation? Her designs verge on the fetishistic but she is in a class of her own and we love her.

So are designer shoes worth it?

I think so – in moderation at least. Well-made shoes *do* last. They are kinder to your feet. And they make you feel a million dollars.

These Boots Were Made for Walking

'These boots are made for walkin'
And that's just what they'll do
One of these days these boots are gonna walk all over you.'

Lee Hazlewood/Nancy Sinatra

There are certain women in the world who will insist on wearing strappy little stilettos all year round. These are the women with unlimited taxi expense accounts or very rich husbands. It still gives me goose bumps every time I see a red-carpet arrival shivering in a skimpy frock and teeny sandals as

Queen Victoria was a big fan of the boot, liking, one presumes, the coverage of the erotic ankle. Sturdy buttoned boots were the norm beneath voluminous crinoline skirts. During the First World War too, boots offered a practical advantage for servicewomen, keeping feet warm and comfortable.

Not until the 1960s did boots become ubiquitous again. Nancy Sinatra's massive hit 'These Boots are Made for Walkin'' confirmed what every fashionable women was already practising. Knee-high boots were the perfect complement to the mini-skirt, block-heeled ankle boots were a liberating change from the restricting stilettos of the 1950s, and designers such as Mary Quant experimented with patent leather, white kid or even clear plastic boots worn over bright jersey tights.

Since the 1970s boots have played a part in the fashion of every decade. Moon-boots enjoyed a brief popularity thanks to the moon landings and Doc Martens became a cult towards the end of the decade. These boots, designed for working men, became immensely popular, worn by everyone from students to revolutionaries, men and women alike; designers customized them in bright colours and acid prints while wearers applied amateur decoration such as floral motifs or Union Jacks. By the 1980s Sloane Rangers were embracing the Chelsea boot, elastic-sided ankle boots favoured by Chelsea mods in the 1960s.

Disco frenzy gave us glitter-laden platform boots and soon the fetishists claimed boots as their own, reaching new heights (literally) in elaborate fastenings, chains and hooks, towering heels, glossy patent finishes and a definite bondage vibe.

Boots are often seen as more erotic than shoes in the way they elongate and caress the leg – particularly those that reach the thigh, revealing a tantalizing bulge of flesh at the top. And being essentially masculine, the bike boot has an element of androgynous sex appeal about it, maybe more so if complemented by a full set of biker leathers. Whatever turns you on, I suppose.

But there are plenty of boots that are simply comfortable and stylish. Riding boots have been in vogue for a few years and, especially when made from soft leather with burnished buckles, are eminently stylish.

Things a Woman Should Know About Shoes

And let's not forget the humble Wellington. Once only available in hunting green, this has become a surprise fashion item, with designers such as Paul Smith and Cath Kidston customizing their own. Flowers, bright colours and recognizable designer prints all make this as serious a fashion statement as anything else – in the city more often than the country.

the temperature struggles above zero.

The more sensible among us, on the other hand, welcome the arrival of winter, knowing we can wave goodbye to waxing bills, inadequate home-pedicures and a host of nasties including blisters and corns. For winter is boot time.

'A soldier in shoes is only a soldier. But in boots he becomes a warrior.'

General Patton

Historically, boots may have been worn by men and women but there is something innately masculine and purposeful about

Things a Woman Should Know About Shoes

striding about with your lower leg encased in leather. Even the most feminine of boots – with pointed toes and delicate heels – encourage us to march rather than softly tread. In this, boots are the antithesis of the stiletto that turns a woman into a masculine-dominated creature who cannot run away. Look at the way boots have crept into the language: 'booted out' or 'get the boot'. No lack of female emancipation there.

As much as shoes, boots are a wardrobe unto themselves. They can be practical, warm and weatherproof in winter or dressy enough for evenings out. On the whole, however, boots are less elegant than shoes. They are also far harder to look stylish in.

Perhaps you spot a pair of boots in a magazine, photographed on the go-on-forever slender legs of this season's hottest model. The clever angle elongates further, making said boots appear to take up a mere third of this Amazon's leg.

If you are wealthy – we are presuming such an advertisement features a designer's most expensive pair, and boots can be twice the price of shoes – you might, if you get on the waiting list early enough, be able to try these boots on.

OK, scrap that scenario. More likely you are on the high street trying on a copycat version that is very like the boots you saw in the magazine but somehow the effect is not *quite* the same. This may be because most women's calves are chunkier than most models' and shoe stores adapt their designs accordingly. Most of us know the agony of trying to force up the zip on a pair of knee-high boots only to have that unsightly bulge below the knee once we do. Why do you think those ugly elasticated-fabric boots became so popular? They fit snugly whatever your leg shape, of course!

As we all know – or should know and take heed from – boots only look as good as the legs that wear them. This is true of boots worn with skirts or boots worn over skinny jeans – please, no, if you have piggy calves and bulging thighs.

One of the few exceptions is a Home Counties-style ensemble of good, solid leather boots worn with a full skirt. This isn't as unfashionable as it sounds if the boots are beautiful burnished tan or darkest chocolate, perhaps with a glint of riding buckle, and the skirt is a well-cut heavy fabric, English-eccentric style. If you are one of those women with a slim torso, tiny waist and heavy pear shape, this is a look guaranteed to flatter – and is a welcome disguise for thick ankles.

With boots it is even more important to buy quality. Cheap boots, maybe because there is so much more of them, just look

Things a Woman Should Know About Shoes

dreadful. And in my experience they break more often, too – zips jam, soles come away, heels fall off.

At one time boots were an office-girl's winter staple. A knee-high pair (often of the unfortunate off-black elasticated variety) were the cold-weather cousin of the court shoe. As I haven't worked in an office for a while I couldn't say if this is still the case, but I will say one thing: no to boots with skirt suits.

Sharp trouser suits with a pair of killer-heeled ankle boots are fine in a 1980s throwback kind of way.

Boots with jeans are good. Cowboy boots with jeans can look great – sexy and chic without trying to hard – but *only* if you get just the right jeans and just the right boots. Slightly battered and faded on both counts.

This is a look you are born to or not. Despite years of yearning, I was not. Too new or worn with any lack of ease on the part of the wearer is fatal.

That takes us to the demise of the boot-leg jean. Apparently this is dead and gone. I don't believe it for a moment. Boot-leg jeans flatter women who are not stick insects. (Not altogether relevant, but interesting: why do you think pregnancy jeans all come in a boot leg?) As 95 percent of us are not stick insects, I think – outside of the unreal world of fashion – boot-leg jeans will survive.

But if you are a slave to fashion do not fear. If you can no longer fit your boots under your new skinny jeans, wear them over. As I said previously, this looks great if you are tall and slim. Perhaps as a slave to fashion you are. The added bonus is that every inch of your boot is on display – gratifying at a sometimes-stratospheric cost.

Ankle boots are rarely a success with skirts or over trousers. Again, fashionistas are exempted. The sliced-low half-shoe, half-boot with the spindly heel that is currently worn with skirts, leggings – you name it – is an example of the boot as fashion statement. Like any other it-shoe, next year you could be cringing.

The kind of ankle boot we all have in our wardrobe, quite probably with chunky heel and side-zip, is useful for height (only if trousers/jeans are long enough to cover, please) and avoiding the problem of what socks/stockings/pop socks (!) to wear with trousers and shoes. (Don't wear tights beneath trousers – very unhygienic).

Things a Woman Should Know About Shoes

Boots with stiletto heels are great for evening – smart spikes under a masculine-style tuxedo, to dress up jeans, etc. But, as with all stilettos, hopeless for day-wear unless you are one of those women who never goes without her extra inches . . . or walks on any surface more challenging than a restaurant carpet.

Biker boots are risky. Again this is the kind of look that a 16-year-old Slovakian model can carry off with sexy aplomb but the rest of us will risk being approached by members of the same sex. If you want something in this vein there are versions replete with buckles and straps but not quite as heavy or chunky as the genuine article.

Last but not least there is the law-unto-itself that is the Ugg boot. Aptly dubbed the Ugly boot (including by myself some years ago), these shapeless, sheepskin Australian inventions are absolute bliss to wear. Like many intrinsically un-stylish items they became a fashion must-have worn by absolutely everyone (their acceptability confirmed by model Kate Moss's obvious love of them), then were declared 'dead'.

But everyone, including Moss, kept on wearing them. So they were hailed as a fashion miracle, that seasonal hit that kept on hitting. Fashion editors condemned them. Women ignored advice and kept on buying. Something so essentially unflattering can hardly be called a classic wardrobe item but – like the Birkenstock sandal – women have real lives, need to walk, run after children and worry about more than the state of their feet. So fashion might forget them but I bet they keep on selling.

Boots offer a spectrum of footwear and styles that is hard to pass up. If you don't have any, buy at least the following:

1) Good-quality knee-high black with an inch or two of heel for wearing with skirts and jeans in winter or, if you are a true brown person, the same in a luxe deep chestnut.

2) A pair of boots suitable for smart dressing – pointed black with a kitten heel is a good option although, like boot-leg jeans, risks looking dated if fashion is your priority.

3) Uggs. So comfortable. So useful. And so much cheaper if ordered direct from Down Under via the website.

Cosy toes

The cult of the Ugg boot took no-one who puts comfort above looks by surprise. Finally fashion was doing the sensible thing and hailing the sheepskin boot as a style item. Kate Moss, Sienna Miller and every other catwalk model trying to get from show to show in time actually *do* value comfort. It isn't models who have chauffeurs and front-row seats. They walk and stand . . . a lot.

Purists say that Uggs should be worn with bare feet. Actually this is blissful although you do feel as if you have ventured out in your slippers. Maybe it is a good idea in the summer (yes, it is surprising how many pairs still strut their stuff when the temperature rises) because anyone who has worn sheepskin boots on even a mild day will realize how warm they keep your feet, especially when walking.

Like all footwear that is essentially boat-like in shape, this kind of boot doesn't offer the best of support. Take a look at the heels of those trendy teenage girls who have perfected the art of the slouchy walk and you will see their Uggs flattened on one side from bad posture, the boot doing nothing to help.

In fact, the slipper-like quality of the Ugg encourages a slap-slap walk, with the foot supporting the boot rather than the other way round, if you see what I mean.

Furthermore, that sheepskin doesn't grip too well, so feet slide around a little inside, which can, over time, cause blisters or calloused heels.

And the last negative – I promise! – is that they are hopeless to keep clean. Mostly made in attractive shades of tan and cream: one puddle and they're ruined. Try spraying with weatherproof guard but accept that too clean is not cool.

All these downsides notwithstanding, I am a big fan. Maybe don't make them your winter staple but for a quick trip out to the corner shop on a Sunday morning they are perfect.

Oh, and like Birkenstocks, they are hopeless for driving in.

The Ugg may be ugly but it is reasonably discreet. The various sheepskin boots hailed by fashion as the 'new Uggs' have never taken off. Kate Moss may still be a fan of her Mukluks but those Navajo markings and swinging tassels are hard to carry off if you are not a supermodel.

In Training

Trainers, love them or hate them, *everyone* wears them. It is not so much do you wear trainers but which trainers do you wear? They are my summer day staples although I confess that, along with Manolo Blahnik, who claims he cannot abide them, I stand by my belief that trainers are the enemy of feminine chic.

In the main, trainers are clumpy, inelegant, either garishly coloured or luminously white and only look passably in keeping with an outfit of jeans and t-shirt. And don't even get me started on the appearance of the work-out shoes MBTs! ('Masai Barefoot Technology', in case you wonder.)

And, to add insult to injury, now designers have jumped on the bandwagon and trainers have as many fashion seasons as any other shoes, the smartest ones aren't even cheap! BUT . . .

•73•

they are blissfully, gloriously comfortable, reasonably good for your feet and, hot new designs notwithstanding, a basic pair is available on the high street for a price we can all afford. So what is a fashion-conscious shoe-buying gal to do?

Wear them, of course. But choose carefully. The only really 'classic' sports shoe is just that. A simple white or off-white canvas pump, no fancy logo, no air sole cushioning, lasts a summer and a little too like walking barefoot but dress-down stylish in a 1950s way. Worn with Capri pants and a wide-brimmed hat, very Euro-chic.

Similarly this kind of shoe will stand in for the ballet pump when nipping around town on your Vespa in a little summer shift or picnicking in the country in full English floral ensemble. A little carried away with the role-playing maybe, but why do you think shops like Cath Kidston, Brora and aristo-country-chic Bamford and Sons carry this kind of shoe?

The other way to go is to adopt the trainer as fashion item. This is expensive, far easier for men to carry off and means your look has to be pure Abercrombie and Fitch casual. It does, however, allow your feet and fashion kudos to benefit equally from all the new technology, design input and brand status the big trainer companies spend millions on.

There is, I have lately discovered, a third way. Only available to girls happy with the English-eccentric, 'I look like I don't give a damn but this outfit took days to get right' method of dressing. Pick a pair of the oldest Dunlops you can find – preferably the ones you played hockey on a muddy field in at boarding school – and adopt a 'What, these old things?' approach to fashion. Yes, you can muddy-up a new pair, but please, please do it convincingly or all street-credibility will be lost.

Some trainer don'ts:

1) Maybe the New York sight of a businesswoman in designer suit rushing off the subway in old trainers, heels in her handbag, is still current, but it smacks of Melanie Griffiths in *Working Girl*, big bouffant hair and 1980s thinking. Practical maybe, stylish never.

2) Trainers with trouser suits. Men do seem to get away with this. Even Sir Paul McCartney I noticed recently. I remember admiring some interior designer in a baggy trouser suit and trainers for her casual chic once – it was circa 1992 and the '80s vibe was not dead.

Things a Woman Should Know About Shoes

3) Orange trainers, glittery trainers (though silver and gold are mysteriously fashionable as I write), platform-heeled trainers and light-up or wheel-attached trainers if you are over the age of ten. (Five for the lights.)

4) Lastly, separate those you wear for sport and those you wear as a shoe. Full-on, high-performance technology for the former, Converse staples (or equivalent) for the latter.

Fashion is unfair on the genders. Mostly women are the lucky ones but in trainer wars it's men. Men love trainers and wear them almost exclusively. Not just real 'sports' trainers but those trendy black leather affairs with a discreet red tag down the back that screams 'Prada'. Even the most classic of English shoe brands, Church's, has a sporty take on the classic black leather lace-up.

I know men with trainer collections reaching into the hundreds. One lovingly labels and stores them in boxes in a way any female shoe-aholic would be proud of. Yes, he is gay, but plenty of straight men have the bug as badly.

Maybe trainer-obsession is a legitimate way to get a masculine fashion fix, but beware – trainers are essentially the preserve of the young and lovely. And that applies to men *far* more than women. If your man has never worn trainers and suddenly comes home in them, suspect a mid-life crisis.

And never let anyone you care about wear trainers, socks and shorts. (N.B. sandals, socks and shorts are no longer a fashion faux pas as long as you are a twenty-something male model or could pass for one.)

The arrival of the trainer, sports shoe, sneaker, whatever you want to call it, as global fashion item is usually placed around the 1970s, both in the USA, where big-budget marketers like Adidas, Reebok and Nike were promoting more than the standard canvas shoe Dunlop and Converse had made for decades, and among Britain's football fans and attitudinal 'yoof'. But the beginnings of this shoe had come a century earlier, when developments in the use of rubber as a sole allowed the creation of a lightweight lawn shoe. Plimsolls became *de rigueur* for children as canvas and rubber were bonded to form the original sports shoe.

Converse All Star, still a globally recognizable brand of sports shoe today, was one of the first to appear, around 1920. It was also the first to appeal across the shoe-buying board, to men, women and children of all social strata, a phenomenon the trainer of today has consolidated.

Between the 1970s and 1990s trainers became big business, with the leading names in the industry such as Nike, Adidas, Reebok and Puma creating shoes for individual sports, using materials other than canvas – including tactile and desirable leather and suede – and enlisting support through collaboration with major sports stars such as basketball's Michael Jordan.

Advances in technology with air support cushioning systems combined with style flairs, such as the transparent window at the back of the shoe, make this a unique blend of form and function and a fashion staple that seems unstoppable. Proof lies in the success of the sports shoes made by designers like Prada (part of its whole Prada Sport diffusion range) and the now-ubiquitous appearance of some kind of 'trainer' in the collections of many major fashion labels.

Summer Season

There was a time – and still is in parts of the world – when man and woman walked barefoot across the land in touch with the earth as nature intended. As an old Persian proverb puts it:

'Tis the same to him who wears a shoe, as if the whole earth were covered in leather.'

We may get a taste of this sensual delight walking barefoot on a sandy beach but, sadly for most of us, even the transition from winter to summer shoe means an agony of blisters and sore feet until our skin adjusts and hardens. Then we complain at how ugly our feet look and rush to the pedicurist for sloughing-off of those hard-won sandal-proofed patches of heel and toe, and the whole cycle starts over again.

Things a Woman Should Know About Shoes

Summer feet are as hard to get right as summer shoes but we never stop trying. Have a professional pedicure if you can possibly afford it. A good one should last you up to six weeks.

If you are confident enough for a DIY version please be patient and take your time; don't do it late at night after too much Chardonnay or ten minutes before you are due to leave for work. Don't EVER be tempted to slap a new coat of varnish over an old one when it starts chipping. It may seem to work for a while, but the effect is no better than painting over wood-chip wallpaper and eventually the layers will fall off, rather like losing a toenail.

Does wearing shoes barefoot ALWAYS hurt? Unfortunately, yes, for a while at least.

As explained in the previous chapters, the most comfortable options are simple white pumps or slip-on driving shoes. Chic, cool and forgiving – there's no need for perfectly painted toes, either.

But these are not as foot-friendly as you might think. Any canvas will give you a blister on first wearing – which, once there, is hell to get rid of. And in terms of unsightliness, plasters poking out of the backs of heels are second only to the horror of a big, fat sticking-plaster twice the width of the leather sandal strap it is trying to protect your foot from. Lovely soft leather driving shoes are my favourite summer staple as they rarely rub, but this is a certain kind of look and it might not be yours.

Consider, too, the beating uncushioned feet get from pavement-pounding all day long. No summer shoes have adequate sole support so you might as well be walking barefoot as far as the pressure on your heels is concerned. There are various recognized medical conditions that feel as if red-hot pins are being inserted into the base of your foot, mostly caused by lack of cushioning. But help is at hand in the form of the plethora of inserts available – cushioned heel or full-foot pads, gel-filled pillows for placing on pressure points – and that is besides corn plasters, cushioned plasters, even special stick-on pads for wearing with heels. We are a delicate lot really.

Flip-flops and other might-as-well-not-be-there sandals

Once upon a very long time ago (round about the time of the Ancient Greeks, actually) it was deemed that the barest strips of leather made the most elegant of foot coverings. Nothing has changed.

Look in any shoe boutique at the start of summer (sorry, by then

it is far too late; try February if you are serious about bagging the season's hottest sandal) and you will see that in the world of summer sandals, the smaller the better. Rather like the fashion industry and celebrity view of the female figure, less is more. No coincidence that strappy sandals look terrible on pudgy feet.

Flat sandals are the real stars of summer. High-heeled sandals are commonplace year-round in the weatherproof, pedicured world of the red carpet.

The most prosaic of fashion designers tend to come over all whimsical when creating summer sandals. As if in relief from all those hard winter boots, harem-style jewel-encrusted strips of leather, metallic finishes, plaits and tassels are all commonplace. Flamboyance on such a small scale is positively encouraged, which is, I suppose, one way to justify the exorbitant cost in relation to the amount of shoe you are buying.

Flip-flops are not immune from glamorizing either. Once only available in plastic, the basic format is often widened at the front and re-invented with expensive leathers and adornments. They can be chic and inexpensive, however. The craze for Brazilian Havianas, for example; at one point dubbed the successor to the Birkenstock (as if that would ever be given up), these are brightly coloured plastic, rather bendy flip-flops with an all-important

DIY Pedicure

Take time.

Soak feet in warm water dosed with essential oil or bath salts. Dry thoroughly and attack with a pumice stone or metal file. (Obviously regular attention of this sort makes the job easier.)

Smooth newly sloughed skin with cream or oil.

Toenails should be clipped straight across and not down the side, which can lead to infection. File as per fingernails.

Cuticles should be pushed back and creamed.

Before applying varnish, separate toes with twisted strips of loo paper, cotton-wool pads or a clever device known as a rubber toe-separator.

Apply base coat, two layers of colour and top coat, and leave to dry AS LONG AS POSSIBLE before putting on shoes or socks. A couple of hours before bed, a barefoot evening and sleeping with feet hanging out should do it.

Don't skimp, file hurriedly (looks ok without polish, terrible once applied) or skip top or base coat. This will last – otherwise you will be touching up within days, which is hard to do invisibly.

discreet branded imprint. But only cost fifteen quid or so.

When I first worked in fashion magazines, a summer staple was those velvet (fake?), woven-soled flip-flops you could buy in Chinese stores. Rather chic in black or deep red, worn with jeans or dresses and accessorized with perfectly polished red nails. (At under ten pounds a pair you could afford a pedi.)

The worry some people have about living in flip-flops for a few months of the year is the giveaway tan-line. (Apart from the terrible things they do to your posture – all that hanging on with the toes – but who cares about that when they are young?) Actually I think the tan-line is a bonus. For a start if

Things a Woman Should Know About Shoes

you are wearing whichever pair of comfortable sandals gave
it to you, no one will see it unless you take them off. And
there is something undeniably sexy about kicking off sandals
to reveal brown and dusty feet made all the more obvious by
those streaks of white across the brow. A bit like admiring your
watch mark. (Was I the only one who did this after the summer
holidays?!)

As summer sandals are so disposable there is less snobbery
about them. Every supermodel, actress or celebrity beauty kicks
around in cheap plastic for a few months of the year. Of course
if you are a world-class beauty it is easy to look cool in plastic.

One warning about a new craze in hippy summer shoes: the
Americans have outdone themselves this time with the arrival of
Crocs. The jury is out. Will they be like Uggs – ugly but cultish
and thus somehow stylish? I can't quite believe these strange,
boat-shaped, to all appearances plastic things (technically they
are a trademarked manmade material called Croslite™), wide
and woven in appearance like those plastic kits little girls take
delight in, will ever be a style classic – but who knows? By all
accounts comfortable, cheap and colourful, they tick a lot of
boxes for a lot of people and, like any cult shoe, have been
widely copied. The new Birkenstock, maybe?

Things a Woman Should Know About Shoes

I have to say the kiddies' versions are kind of cute but I don't think I'll be rushing out to buy a pair, despite the numerous new styles flooding the market daily. I am somewhat sceptical of the claims that they are a super-shoe and the answer to all our foot problems – in summer at least. Manufacturers claim that the patented material is *better* than a natural fibre, odour resistant, anti-bacterial and anti-fungal, not to mention the orthopaedically correct design with portholes to keep air circulating and feet fresh. Unfortunately there has been such a massive debate on whether they are the answer to our prayers or the worst style crime in recent history that I would probably steer clear of them even if I did like the way they looked. Grudgingly I admit that they would be useful poolside though.

Androgyny

Men have rather lucked out on the shoe front . . . or have they? Instead of a daily headache about which shoes to wear with which outfit, whether feet and back can stand heels or if a fat bottom is a price worth paying for the comfort of flats, men are limited to loafers, lace-ups or trainers.

Of course loafers can be soft, Italian and dandy, or solid, English burnished burgundy. Lace-ups range from the sporty rubber-soled to the highly polished gentleman's brogue. And boots are an acceptable substitute for shoes under most trouser types. Of all these, however, it is the brogue that is most gentlemanly, least unisex and therefore most covetable to the modern, stylish woman.

Things a Woman Should Know About Shoes

From Ancient Greece and throughout Renaissance times, shoes for men and women were not dissimilar – in fact men, particularly those of status, were likely to wear the more flamboyant designs. Since the beginning of the twentieth century, however, men's shoes have become more conservative while exotic women's designs have flourished.

In the early part of the twentieth century, nonetheless, many women's shoes were a modification of men's. Take the boots worn by women in the 1920s – utilitarian, practical and not dissimilar to the boots men had worn in the trenches of the First World War a few years earlier.

The brogue, however, did not cross the gender divide until the 1930s, when Hollywood legend Katharine Hepburn adopted her trademark look – effortlessly stylish and somehow sexy in its androgyny – of baggy mannish trousers and polo-neck sweater set off by traditional English brogues. Similarly, the shoes sported by Coco Chanel when she popularized trousers for women's sporting and country lifestyles in the 1930s were not dissimilar to the brogue. Aside from the

trademark stitching, and often in white or cream, these somewhat less structured lace-ups were the perfect foil to Chanel's feminized take on men's clothes: wide-legged, high-waisted trousers, topped off with a striped sweater, a neat jersey top and ropes of pearls lest anyone forget her femininity.

Another advocate of men's clothes – and a wearer of a trademark string of pearls – was Vita Sackville-West. The famed writer, gardener and lesbian (though she had a long and successful marriage with two sons) wore, particularly in her more reclusive and eccentric later years, breeches, a man's jacket and custom-made, knee-high gardening boots as she strode around her estate.

Today the popularity of androgynous clothing – women's tuxedos for evening wear, ubiquitous jeans and free borrowing of boyfriends' clothes – has not often extended to men's shoes. But there is something indisputably chic about these shoes that has led shoe designers such as Emma Hope and stalwart men's-shoe stores such as Church's to create brogues for women.

There is no doubt that some shoes appear unisex; Converse trainers, Birkenstocks and driving shoes are identical in design despite their intended gender. But can women actually wear men's shoes of the more formal, old-fashioned school?

Well, not really. Men's feet tend to be not only longer but wider than women's. So a size 40 for men is bigger than for women. For those with cash to spare and a quirky desire for a traditional pair of handmade shoes, there is no reason at all why a traditional men's shoe-maker such as John Lobb could not be persuaded to make a perfectly fitted pair of men's shoes for a woman. Excellent for the feet, too.

When it comes to a shoe such as the brogue, part of the charm in seeing it on a woman is a discreet feminizing of the essential design: elongating the toe and narrowing the shape, for example. It is rather like the difference between wearing *actual* men's jeans, complete with roomy crotch, and 'boyfriend'-style jeans. Similarly a tailored jacket, albeit blazer-style, would be far too wide on the shoulder (not to mention buttoning on the wrong side) for a woman to wear without looking slightly odd.

This leads us to the question of which shoes to wear with androgynous-style clothing?

As in all things, it is a matter of what kind of shoe suits what kind of outfit or more specifically what occasion. A pair of wide-legged mannish trousers goes best with plain pumps and a neatly fitted top for casual summer dressing. Swap canvas plimsolls for leather brogues and add a men's-style suit jacket, and the outfit is smarter and pure Katharine Hepburn. A tuxedo, on the other hand, although stolen from the male wardrobe, undoubtedly works best Helmut Newton-style: narrow-legged, unsparingly fitted and finished off with killer heels.

To conclude, then, women should take inspiration from the wardrobes of their men but choose actual garments with great caution. And leave the shoes. Apart from the strange confidence crisis your relationship might undergo when it is revealed that you share a shoe-size (far worse for the male ego than sharing a waist size), men don't care for their feet the way we do. Their shoes smell, they crumble; they wear them down by walking badly . . . need I go on?

(Actually, you shouldn't borrow shoes from anyone and certainly NEVER buy them second-hand. Shoes are quickly moulded to their owner's foot-shape, making it difficult to switch wearer. Not to mention the bacteria all that sweat encourages.)

Knit Your Own Sandals

Before you dismiss shoes as a necessity turned frivolous fashion, think again – shoes are a political issue. Well, not shoes per se, but leather. Though not quite as controversial as wearing fur, increasingly, for a growing segment of the population, making shoes from animal skins is unacceptable.

Shoes are, of course, traditionally made from skin: cow, pig, snake, crocodile, you name it. In the beginning this was for good reason; leather is hard, durable and good for protecting our own delicate skin. Suede, the flipside, is soft, sensual and alluring – all the attributes a discerning man or woman of taste wants from a fashionable item of footwear.

Today the variety of animal skins used to make shoes is staggering. And though designers would rarely risk using an endangered species the question remains – why use leather at all?

Before you squirm uncomfortably over your tofu salad, take heart, there are plenty of vegetarians who are perfectly comfortable with wearing leather. Perhaps this is because for a long time being ethical and being chic were mutually exclusive.

That was before Stella McCartney. The daughter of campaigning vegetarian Linda McCartney, she is one of the few celebrities who has actually practised what she preaches and created a line of top-end designer shoes with prices to match those of her exclusive clothes. And if you think it is a bit of a gamble charging hundreds of pounds for shoes made in suedette, canvas or raffia, think again: these shoes have design kudos and a conscience – priceless! How could the fashion industry resist? Well, of course, those who decide what is fashionable and what is not couldn't resist the opportunity to wear their consciences on their feet, and made sure that everyone knew about Stella's vegan shoe policy to maximize the feelgood factor, every man, woman and beast a winner.

But what about your average vegetarian or vegan without a wallet to match designer price-tags? Are they condemned to a

lifetime of plastic shoes in muddy colours and clumpy designs? Google 'vegan shoes' on the internet and you will be staggered by the number of sites that come up. Ethical footwear – and increasingly ethical clothing – is big business. Acknowledging your carbon footprint is not enough anymore, you need to take responsibility for your *actual* footprint too.

Birkenstocks have long been the hippy's favourite and since their new-found fashion status they are the obvious choice for an inexpensive, ethical, comfortable and fashionable shoe. Be sure, however, to make the right choice. Birkenstocks come with leather or man-made uppers but the regular (and most popular) multi-coloured man-made versions have a standard suede inner lining. They do also make a dedicated vegan shoe with a textile lining – so make sure you pick the right one! What is more, as a company they are fairly unimpeachable, having been eco-conscious for the past 30 years and working hard on energy economy.

So sandals are catered for. Birkenstock also make plenty of other shoes but they are an acquired taste with their super-foot- (and earth-) friendly wide, round shape. I saw an orange-clad Buddhist monk wearing a pair the other day and they suited his outfit perfectly. Other makers' shapes veer further in the clog direction, and materials such as polyurethane are hardly

Things a Woman Should Know About Shoes

inspiring from a fashion or a foot-comfort point of view. Microfibre is pretty good these days and said to breathe as well as leather, and canvas (organic cotton or hemp for the truly worthy) is eco-friendly enough. Overall, however, you have to be pretty dedicated to sacrifice fashion sensibilities for good conscience. There is a worrying predominance of unflattering boat-like shapes around; perhaps all those vegetables encourage foot-widening?

Sorry, no mockery intended, and in fact shapes like these are far, far healthier and in line with what nature intended our feet to look like that your average pair of narrow ballerina pumps. Ever tried walking barefoot, even just for the length of your summer holiday, and then squeezing into narrow shoes? It takes worryingly little time for your feet to relax, slump and spread!

So, knitting your own shoes may not be such a bad idea after all – all those front-row fashion queens with their knitting needles stashed in their Luella bags might know something we don't.

Slip into Something More Comfortable

The term 'slipper' is somewhat of a misnomer. Think of Dorothy's ruby slippers in *The Wizard of Oz*, for example – hardly the kind of shoe you would want to squeeze bed-warm feet into on a chilly winter's morning.

Dictionary definitions of the word employ terms such as 'light', 'low-cut' and 'usually worn around the house', although lexicologists seem to think that dancing is a popular pursuit for slipper-wearers. 'Casual' is another word to describe the slipper and, obviously, the derivation is from the way the shoe is 'slipped on'.

Slip into Something More Comfortable

Semantics apart, the slipper has to be *comfortable*. Whether it is being worn sloppily around the house or for an evening where feet will touch nothing but plush carpeting, the word 'slipper' conjures up soft fabrics like velvet and suede, cream soles never intended to go outside and a certain decadence. This is a shoe for feet that do no work.

Unfortunately these days a slipper is more likely to be made from velour and sport a cartoon of Bart Simpson. And don't even get me started on those enormous animal heads that perfectly sane grown-ups feel it is appropriate to wear indoors. Of course what you choose to wear when in your own home is no one else's business, but consider this: why would any woman dedicated to owning as many pairs of shoes as possible pass up the opportunity for a whole new world of footwear? Furthermore, if you care about looking chic and elegant – or funky and fashionable – in daily life, why (nostalgia apart) would you slap your feet into a stinky pair of fluffy animal slippers you have had since you were a teenager and wearing Mickey Mouse t-shirts to bed?

There is a certain type of woman – a self-styled girl's girl – who favours ultra-feminine dresses, strappy heels and coquettish glances. As if to offset her seductive public persona this same woman, at home alone – or better still watching *Bridget Jones's*

Things a Woman Should Know About Shoes

Diary for the twentieth time with other single girlfriends – will wear sweat-clothes or pyjamas and slippers aimed at the pre-teen girl market. You guessed it: pink, fluffy or, sorry to go on about it, those floppy-eared animal heads again. Don't you trip over the ears on your way to get more Ben and Jerry's from the freezer?

Forget them. At night you might wear a silk negligee or a vintage white cotton nightie; your boyfriend's old t-shirts or nothing at all. Slippers should match. (By the way, you will look pretty silly wearing nothing but a pair of slippers, no matter how nice they are. Invest in underfloor heating is my advice.)

And on other occasions that call for slipper-wearing – house-parties, holidays, even hospital visits – make yourself feel good and wear something decent. Although I admit I may have gone too far (unintentionally) when I gave birth in a pair of £150 Italian cashmere slippers.

Cashmere slippers, like cashmere dressing-gowns, bed-socks and hot-water bottles, are the height of decadence. They are absurdly indulgent, hopelessly impractical and, given daily use, last no time at all before turning to fluff and holes. Yet somehow, feeling that special every morning and evening is worth it.

Any luxury fabric will have the same effect, although cashmere (or good wool) is lovely to put cold feet into, unlike leather slippers that may look smart but feel slimy and unforgiving against bare feet. Velvet or satin is usually just used on an upper and the shoe itself lined in leather, so same problem applies, though these are very elegant as evening dress slippers.

Sheepskin is delicious against bare skin – hence the theory that Ugg boots should be worn barefoot. Ugg actually make slippers now but, as with all sheepskin slippers, they aren't that attractive on the feet; but they're not a bad option for warmth and comfort – the two most important considerations.

Slippers are, by definition, for slipping feet into, so backless versions are great, plus they make that satisfying slap-slap as they flop down against the floor that is so good when mooching around the house. Less comfortable but undoubtedly glamorous are mules. I don't know anyone who actually wears those marabou-trimmed pink, satin affairs, but then I don't really move in that kind of social circle. Whether they are comfortable or not I don't know, but if you fancy a little 1950s glamour, why not? Marilyn Monroe would have done.

Slippers are not just the things you wear to the bathroom and back. In this age of stilettos that ruin parquet flooring, cream-

Things a Woman Should Know About Shoes

coloured carpets that show every speck of dirt and the *House & Garden* pressure for everything to look perfect, many people leave outdoor shoes at the front door. It reminds me of being at school, aged around eight, when indoor and outdoor shoes were required. Mind you, so were inner and outer pairs of knickers.

A pair of soft leather slip-ons to replace dirty or, more likely, uncomfortable shoes when you come in is a sensible idea. Bring back the pipe-and-slippers regime – for women as well as men. They need not be actual bedroom slippers but any pair of loafers too worn to stand daily pavement-beating, or a dedicated leather-upper, suede-sole combination. Classic men's shoe-makers are the places to find these and often do a women's version as well as a men's.

Having decided to leave working shoes at the front door, it is worth thinking about leaving something at the back too. The thought of gardening shoes might make you smirk but a pair of clogs to slip into for a stolen ten minutes of morning sun is not such a bad idea. And if you are lucky enough to live in the country or have a big garden, wellies lined up by the door are practical and, looking at shots in the glossy magazines, an interior-design statement too – line up in height order, please.

Perfect Posture

High heels may make you look and feel fantastic but there is a price to pay. And back treatment doesn't come cheap.

The problem with wearing high heels – and to a lesser extent any shoe that changes the natural shape of your foot – is that your feet are literally the foundation of your body, determining your balance, your movement and the way the entire rest of your body works. As my Alexander-technique teacher explained to me, high heels push your body weight forward, so to stop yourself toppling you have to use your muscles – many in the lower back – to push yourself back again. These muscles are not intended to work this way nor have they had much practice doing so.

Advice on how to walk in heels includes focusing on putting

your weight on your heels, not the balls of your feet, but this immediately makes you sway-backed. Compensating by tucking your tail in just makes even more muscles work harder and against nature. (Although flatter tummies have sometimes been reported.)

You may have put the aches and pains of a 'morning after' down to one-too-many but blame your shoes as well! The pain in your calves after staggering home from a nightclub still wearing your heels will rival the most ruthless step-aerobics class. And it isn't just backs that suffer from poor posture: necks shorten, shoulders tighten, our breathing becomes shallower than ever, knees buckle, ankles weaken. Are you put off yet?

Of course not, because, as women all know, 'no pain, no gain,' and if heels make you look and feel great a little backache is a small price to pay – within reason. Actually, even Alexander practitioners aren't totally anti-heels. My teacher has me put blocks under both the front and the back of my feet to experience the difference that tipping the body backwards and forwards does to your posture – a worthwhile exercise that might actually make it easier for you to walk (occasionally) in heels. As in all things, awareness of your movement and posture is key.

Things a Woman Should Know About Shoes

It might be worth mentioning the new craze for shoes that supposedly make us walk the way nature intended, MBTs ('Masai Barefoot Technology') being the most well known. These trainer-type shoes are built up at the front to push your body weight back onto your heels – in the style of the Masai people of East Africa, the blurb maintains. The effect on your thighs is similar to a hard week's skiing. But, as with all forced changes, your lower back may suffer from such an exaggerated change in posture. Use with caution, even if they do give your thighs a mega workout.

There are, of course, high heels and there are *really* high heels. I'm talking the mythological six inches – it does exist actually but probably as many transvestites wear them as women. (Pedantically there is good reason for this: men have bigger feet, therefore it is easier for them to walk in super-high heels as their weight is not pushed as far forward.)

If you think adding a couple of inches won't make that much difference, think again. Just because you spend your days tripping down the road atop a three-inch kitten (heel, no animal rights protestors here, thank you), that doesn't mean walking in a 'dangerous-weapon stiletto' is going to be easy. After all, it takes years for ballet dancers to master *en pointe*.

And if your feet are any smaller than a size six or seven forget six-inch heels. (Bear in mind in heels you will probably go up a size or two anyway.) Tipping yourself onto your toes just isn't an option unless you want to risk serious injury and possible surgery. If you put on a pair of heels and you can't balance on the ball of your foot, put them back, even (unlikely) if they are a free pair of Manolos. Back!

The wearing of very high heels is risky and, given that most women cannot achieve a graceful walk in a pair, not really worth it. Unless you are a budding dominatrix why risk the agony of shortened calf muscles, throwing your back out or, and it is a risk, deep vein thrombosis?

It is rather like the comment a boy I really liked made to me when I was trying to smoke a cigarette in my teens: apparently I looked stupid. Why risk harming yourself when you look silly in the process?

It is impossible to drive a car, walk on grass, in mud or even on a cobbled street in these shoes. As Naomi Campbell famously proved, even models who spend a lifetime practising aren't immune to the odd tumble.

Things a Woman Should Know About Shoes

So, stick to four inches max. Three inches is high enough for most women and a sufficient boost to height and confidence to completely alter the way you feel. Practise a bit at home, work up inch-by-inch and do a few foot-stretching exercises – heel-wearing being a well-known athletic activity – and you will be fine.

The way a pair of heels changes you is not just physical, you see; it is as much, if not more, of a psychological boost. We women have such fragile self-esteem (on some occasions, at least) that even small things such as wearing a sexy dress, brighter lipstick or higher heels than normal are enough to make you feel like a new woman. Clichéd but true.

Heels make you taller, therefore they make you thinner (!) and with a bit of practice they give you a confident walk – sexy or powerful depending on the situation.

'Stiletto, I look at it more as an attitude as opposed to a high-heeled shoe.'

Lita Ford

No Pain No Gain

Any shoe can hurt your feet.

Even the ones that are supposed to be comfortable.

Especially the ones that are supposed to be comfortable – when they are new, at least.

Unfortunately shoes come in standard sizes but feet don't. That means that even when you wear a pair of correctly sized, orthopaedic-approved lace-ups made from soft leather, with moulded heels and support inner-soles, you may well end up with blisters. Leather may turn soft and supple in the long run, but it is almost always stiff before it is worn a bit, so be prepared for any shoe to fight back before it has moulded to the shape of your foot.

Things a Woman Should Know About Shoes

There are, however, plenty of shoes far less humble than a comfortable slip-on that demand your foot moulds to them, not the other way round. Personify the pointed-toe high-heeled pump, give it a snooty accent, and there is no way this shoe is going to ruin its silhouette by allowing your feet to assume their natural shape.

Unfortunately in most cases of pointed shoes (high-heeled or flat) both the foot *and* the shoe are ruined. In a furious tug-of-war your feet push and push against the front of such a shoe but at the point at which the shoe begins to narrow (the same point at which your foot is widest, unfortunately) the shoe fights back. The result is a nasty bulge, because no matter how much the leather stretches, feet will never taper to a point, so bunions, corns, blisters and in the long term deformed toes are the price you have to pay.

Logically, buying a bigger size should help, the point coming further down your foot, but unfortunately this only results in ugly toe-cleavage and heels that slip off at the back. Bunions front, blisters back – hopeless.

And there is no getting away from the agony of the heel. Arches were not designed to be elevated so far off the ground; think of the pain a ballerina goes through, and take one look at a dancer's feet and your childhood *Swan Lake* fantasy will be over forever. The balls of our feet are simply not designed to carry our full weight, and the rest of our body loyally joins in the protest.

Discomfort, however, is just the start of it. There is a whole world of Nasties that lurk below. Here are just a few:

Blisters: minor but irritating, blisters occur when feet get hot and sweaty and skin rubs against foot or shoe. Fluid then fills up between the layers of skin to protect it. RESIST popping a blister if it hasn't done so by itself as this can cause infection. The fluid will reabsorb and the skin will heal on its own.

Bunions: clichéd but a surprisingly common foot deformity, a bunion is caused when the bone of the big toe becomes displaced and it starts to move towards your middle toes. The bunion is a bony protrusion on the side of the joint. In severe cases the big toe may even move beneath or overlap the second toe. The most common cause is ill-fitting footwear. Unsurprisingly more women suffer from this condition than men.

A bunion is most painful when wearing the tight shoes that caused it, as it can make the foot widen. Redness, swelling and pain are just the beginning. **Hammer-toe** at the second toe may follow when it is pushed in so that it contracts and curls under to further press on a shoe. A corn on top is likely.

Calluses: these are essentially just areas of hard skin caused by pressure. Ill-fitting and high-heeled shoes are culprits but standing for too long and being overweight exacerbate the problem. Moisturize, remove with a pumice stone and avoid high heels or thin soles. Never try to remove hard skin yourself with a razor blade or pair of scissors (yikes!). Cushioning pads for heels, soles or the whole foot can be a big help.

Corns: pressure from shoes or walking causes the skin to thicken and form a hard central core. The pain comes from inflammation, swelling and pressure around the core. Silicone pads are a better alternative to corn plasters, which can affect healthy skin, but the only solution may be to stop wearing the offending shoes, at least for a while.

Cracked heels: mostly this is a cosmetic problem caused by dry skin or conditions such as eczema and psoriasis but also by open-backed shoes, especially very flat ones with thin soles. It can worsen and become painful if the fissures deepen and start to bleed. To avoid the problem, moisturize regularly, especially after bathing.

Things a Woman Should Know About Shoes

Heel pain and spurs: summer feet suffer from inadequately cushioned soles, resulting in pain and inflammation of the heel and arch of the foot. At worst this may develop into a spur when excess calcium deposits cause a bony protrusion that can be extremely painful. Depending on the extremity of the case, treatment may involve inner-soles for cushioning, anti-inflammatory treatment and even, as a last resort, surgery.

Ingrowing nails: this is a potentially very painful complaint that needs specialist attention from a chiropodist. Injury to the foot may cause acute in-growth where the toe is red, swollen and agonizing to the touch, and may discharge pus or even blood. Tight shoes can be a cause but so can cutting your toenails the wrong way; avoid cutting down the sides of the nail, just trim straight across the top.

Sweaty, smelly feet: not so much a poor-shoe condition but perhaps exacerbated by wearing no socks and/or man-made fibres. Aside from the obvious social embarrassment this condition can cause, patches of skin may peel and become painful or athlete's foot could occur.

Athlete's foot is a fungal infection that can occur anywhere on the body but is often found between the toes, in the form of very itchy, either dry and peeling or soggy white skin. It is nasty and can spread, so treat it fast. Anti-fungal powders can be used in socks and shoes, and sprays or creams should knock it on the head – but beware, if you are sweaty you are prone to a repeat bout. Avoid bare feet in shoes (particularly closed, man-made fibres such as trainers) and wear cotton socks, changed regularly. Teenage boys take note!

Verrucae: similar to corns but not as big, verrucae (or verrucas) are almost flat, with tell-tale black dots. (Remember wondering what they were as a child? Actually they are small blood vessels feeding the verruca.) They are not really painful but resist trying to squeeze them out as this will be painful and cause them to spread – they are easily transferred by touch. Treat with localized cream or ointments.

Are you feeling sick yet?

Feet are one of the most neglected parts of the body, stuffed into tights, socks and shoes – and even when something goes wrong we tend to ignore it. Not a pleasant exercise, but spend a few moments looking down at other people's feet in summer and you might be horrified: horny, yellowing, fungal nails, pulsating red bunions, plasters masking blisters and heels resembling a parched river bed are but a few of the delights of exposing our feet.

Things a Woman Should Know About Shoes

There is a whole world of footcare out there, we just don't make it a priority. Time to change.

Podiatry

This is the term that is increasingly coming to replace chiropody for the medical treatment of the foot and ankle. Podiatrists are professionals who undergo long training similar to that of a doctor, and treatment (mostly in the US) can be surgical. Make an appointment with them for professional nail-cutting, the removal of corns or calluses, advice on shoes and how to modify them with orthotic devices if appropriate. A general one-stop shop for foot health.

Pedicure

Podiatry is for real foot-health problems; a pedicure will answer cosmetic ones. Nails will be clipped and filed, dead skin removed, the surface polished and buffed and a pretty colour applied. If you have a nail disorder or disease that cannot be treated, advice will be given and referral to a specialist encouraged. Massage is often part of the treatment and if, like me, you love your feet being touched this is pure bliss. I am told that an equal number of people cannot bear their feet to be

touched or are so ticklish they simply cannot stand it. Unlucky for some as a pedicure is both a feel-good and look-good pampering exercise for healthy but unsightly feet.

Reflexology

This complementary branch of foot treatment is lovely for the feet but is actually far more holistic, having far-reaching effects across the whole body. (Interesting point – if you have a fractured foot or a verruca that precludes reflexology on the feet, it can be done on hands and even ears!)

Reflexologists believe that areas on the foot correspond to areas of the body and that stimulation of certain points can help self-healing. It is usually a lovely experience although certain points can be extremely sensitive, indicating possible problems in the body. In my experience this is usually that perverse 'good' pain like the pummelling of hard knots in the shoulders during a back massage. While reflexology won't make your feet fit your shoes any better, it does give you some respect for the foot at least, plus it is a relaxing, stress-relieving treatment that can have positive effects for your whole body.

A Step Too Far

'If the shoe doesn't fit, must we change the foot?'

Gloria Steinem

Gloria Steinem's remark may have been made in jest but over the centuries a surprising number of cultures have endorsed barbaric practices such as foot binding in the name of feminine beauty.

Extreme beauty has not had its day, however. Cosmetic surgery is now commonplace on almost all parts of the body, including the feet. So-dubbed 'foot facelifts' include operations to shave and shorten claw toes, which overhang the big toe (incompatible with pointed shoes!), surgically remove bunions and inject the balls and pads of the feet with collagen in order to make high-heel-wearing more comfortable.

Banned in 1912, the Chinese practice of foot binding started in the tenth century and had become widespread by the twelfth century, first among the upper classes and eventually among all but the poorest of women, who were needed to work in the fields.

Legend has it that the practice originated among the concubines to the Emperor and soon spread to other concubines and then throughout the social strata. Tragically, by the seventeenth century, despite attempts to abolish the custom, the feet of girls as young as four or five were being bound tightly. The process involved breaking all but the big toe of the child and applying layers of tightly wrapped bandages, initially changed every couple of days. The subsequent bending of the foot arch aimed to achieve the ideal three-inch 'gold lotus' foot. The 'silver lotus' of four inches was the maximum allowed.

The side-effects of such an extreme process were mainly caused by widespread infection. In-growing toenails, for instance, in some cases led to such flesh-rotting that the toes died and dropped off. Disease often followed, and death was not uncommon. The binding took place over a period of up to ten years of agonizing pain. In later life women were so disabled that for some walking was impossible, and falls and broken bones were frequent consequences.

The deformities caused by the practice of Chinese foot binding are brought to mind as we read stories of women who need the bones of their feet re-set after years of wearing inappropriate high-heeled and pointed-toed shoes.

Are you put off yet?

You should be: foot surgery of this sort carries higher risks of long-term problems than many other cosmetic improvements. You don't, after all, walk around on your face all day.

Infection, nerve-injury and even injecting fillers could make walking difficult and painful in the long run. Foot bones may become floppy or misaligned and, as any Alexander technique teacher will tell you, problems in the foot soon become problems in the back, hips and neck. Ironically, surgery undergone to make wearing restricting shoes more comfortable could backfire, leaving ugly support shoes as the only option.

Generally I am not a big fan of cosmetic surgery – always reserving a woman's prerogative to change her mind (as she gets older and saggier!). But while the thought of smoothing out a few wrinkles, lifting the bust or lipo-ing out some baby fat is understandable, if a little horrifying, to actually go as far as surgery simply in order to wear heels seems extraordinary. Although I suppose women have liposuction to fit into tight trousers, so why not to fit into tight heels?

Cosmetic foot surgery is just more proof that the world is going mad. Well, maybe just a certain type of woman's world.

The bottom line is that if you can bear the discomfort they cause for a couple of hours, the shoes you have stuffed your feet into can't be that bad. If you have to chop a bit of bone off, have re-constructive surgery, undergo weeks of pain (and not being able to wear shoes at all, one presumes) – not to mention the vast cost – in order to wear your shoes of choice, a word of advice: get new shoes.

Life is too short.

So Your Feet Don't Get Fat?!

Many times – and with many friends – I have consoled myself that while our bodies may have become too bulgy for designer dresses, our feet still happily believed we were a size ten and dainty designer shoes agreed.

Some of us are lucky enough to keep slim, elegant feet that may not necessarily match the rest of our physiques, but as our bodies thicken with age so, most often, do our feet. Unfairly, even if you manage to starve yourself into staying slim as you hit 40 or even 50, your feet will probably rebel. And all those 'investment shoes' tucked in the back of the wardrobe, those never worn but 'such a bargain in the sale' shoes don't fit

any more!! (It has been known for feet to slim down a width fitting, if not in length, from dramatic weight loss but this is quite unusual.) The fact of the matter is that feet spread as you grow older. Hardly surprising really – imagine even an average woman's weight bearing down over a long period of time. And, to add insult to injury, as you age those fat deposits – happy to take up home everywhere else on your body – start to thin out on your feet. Losing those pads of cushioning makes wearing any shoes less comfortable, particularly those that weren't that comfortable in the first place.

Given that once you pass a certain age your sense of balance can play up and – particularly if you are a post-menopausal woman – falling could have dire consequences for your bones, why do you think you see so few older women in serious heels? Joan Collins excepted, of course.

'Ha!' you might say. Those problems are *years* off, as you trip along to the nearest designer-shoe sale to pick up a few more pairs of stilettos. Had any children yet?

Pregnancy takes its toll on the body in many ways but one that women don't always know about is the foot-spreading problem. Increased blood volume in the body (by as much as 40 percent), fluid retention and weight gain can make feet and ankles swell during pregnancy, which in turn leads to some women needing larger shoes. A friend went up two shoe sizes in her first pregnancy. Rather unfortunately, after the baby was born she only went down one size, despite regaining her flawless figure.

Before you panic, this doesn't happen to all of us. I did wear my Manolo Blahnik stilettos to a party three weeks before my son was due – and quite comfortably. Unfortunately a few years of running after a small boy in nothing but 'comfortable shoes' and those same Manolos are beginning to feel just a *little* tight. And hands up, I admit I am sitting here writing this, six months pregnant with my second, and unable to wear anything but Birkenstocks with comfort.

(Slightly off the point but if you are pregnant and *haven't* experienced any swelling round the foot, as I didn't, don't panic when a day or so after the birth all the extra fluid you have been carrying for nine months disperses itself downwards. For a day you will have the puffy feet and ankles of your worst nightmares!)

A combination of age and life makes widening feet commonplace. The first shoe casualties to fall from your wardrobe will probably be pointed ones. Next to go are heels in the daytime – though on the odd night out a few extra inches are so good for our self-esteem that a little discomfort is a small price to pay.

Last but not least, there will be certain favourites that were once your most comfortable shoes but are bulging at the sides or your toes are touching the end. This tends to be more of a problem in summer when your feet are apt to swell anyway.

Of course the thing we tend to forget is that our tolerance for discomfort also lessens with age. Sometimes, due to persistent foot problems like bunions or corns, wearing some shoes becomes unbearably uncomfortable, but there comes a time when even if you could bear mildly uncomfortable shoes, you don't want to.

Life is too short.

I don't want to worry about having plasters available in case blisters develop. I am always in a hurry so need shoes I can walk fast in, and my income has dropped to a level where daily taxi usage is unthinkable. Get the picture?

So, take a fond look at all those shoes in your collection that may never be worn again. You can always put them in an arty display case so that they can still be admired.

And take heart – your shoes may no longer fit but you *really* are never too fat for your handbag.

Taxi, Please

When, straight out of university and broke, I started work at Vogue House, I was justifiably terrified about my daily working wardrobe. One look at the shoe collection in the fashion cupboard and the thing I worried most about was getting my shoes right. But I took the bus to work. And the bus stop was ten minutes' walk away. And as general dogsbody I was back and forth up the stairs, to the photocopier and down to the post room buried in the basement. Worst of all, I was broke.

So as for taxis. . . without an expense account, forget it.

Luckily it was winter; knee-high, flat boots with the look of Wellingtons about them were in fashion and, let's face it, nobody noticed me anyway. But this is an example of the way in which shoes have to fit in with your lifestyle.

Episodes of *Sex and the City* may picture Sarah Jessica Parker tripping down the steps of a New York brownstone and off to coffee with the girls in four-inch stilettos but few women can pull this off in real life. Even if they are on the petite side and need the physical and psychological boost. Not unless they want to ruin their feet by the time they are 40.

Ms Parker may only have to walk to the end of the street before the director calls cut, but unless you have a taxi waiting outside your front door, forget daily heel wearing. If you drive everywhere, you can put your heels on when you arrive, but *don't* drive in them. Keep some aptly named 'driving shoes', aka Tods-style loafers, in the car.

Here are a few questions to ask yourself if you find your shoe-identity isn't quite tallying with reality or, worse, if you go from sleek professional to full-time mother without a wardrobe update on the way:

1) How much do you walk? Regular hikes of over a mile and your shoes need to be ultra-comfortable – trainers, cushion-soled loafers, well-fitting boots with barely-there block heel, moulded sandals etc. Also, make sure all your footwear is worn in.

(Interesting aside – I read recently that there is no such thing as 'wearing in' shoes and they should be comfortable from the moment you put them on. For the record I *completely* disagree. Almost all my shoes have niggled a little for the first wearings.)

2) How much do you care about comfort? Again, if you really don't want to think about your shoe choice when you get dressed – or if your worst nightmare is painful feet – go for some of the easy-to-walk-in options above. There is no reason you can't be stylish in simple Parisien-chic loafers, trendy trainers or, though not very supportive, ballet pumps, depending on your style.

3) What is the state of your back? If you have *any* back problems choose support. So while trendy flip-flops or a pair of boots with two-inch-high block heels are comfortable enough for walking for some people, for others (me included) they are a one-way ticket to the osteopath's couch.

4) How much do you carry? (Or, without being rude, how much do you weigh?) If you lug a two-kilo (five-pound) handbag, masses of shopping or a small child around with you regularly, give your feet a break and choose shoes with enough width. Similarly, in summer feet swell.

Things a Woman Should Know About Shoes

5) Who do you need to impress? There may come a time in life when, important as it is to wear clothes and shoes that make you feel good about yourself, you are seeing no one but other mothers on the school run. And while some would say they are the hardest to impress, is it really worth sacrificing foot health for image? It is? Then over-sized sunglasses and a designer handbag are wonderful school-gate weapons.

6) And if you simply have to wear heels for work everyday, do as the Americans do (ugly as it is) and wear trainers with your suit while you walk and keep your heels for carpeted offices and taxis.

None of the above means you need to give up wearing impractical shoes ever. But the odd evening when a stunning pair of shoes will really make a difference isn't going to cause you foot problems in the long run.

The biggest worry is what your shoes say about you . . . .

Super-high, sexy stilettos in daytime: footballer's wife or call girl.

Beaten-up ballet flats, flip-flops or squashed Ugg boots: student or model.

Caramel-coloured loafers (with matching bag), plain white pumps, smart knee-high boots: American investment-banker's wife in London.

Jewelled sandals, animal-print pumps, patent boots: Eurotrash.

Old trainers, pink Birkenstocks, Scuffed LK Bennet flats: harassed mothers.

It's a minefield out there!

If the Shoe Fits . . .

'You cannot put the same shoe on every foot'

Pubilius Syrus

The above (tongue-in-cheek!) guide to quite what your shoes say about you is one way of deciding what impression you want to put across, but for most of us just finding ones that fit is hard enough.

Bespoke shoes may be beyond the realms of most people's wallets but there is something to be said for buying the best quality you can afford, even off the peg. And while for the sartorially exacting or those with problem feet a couture pair may be necessary, for most of us it is possible, with a little (enjoyable) research, to find a style and brand that suits our feet. For example, my feet are reasonably long and not too broad but somehow my toes never lived up to the long elegance of my fingers, making all those long, narrow-tipped styles impossible. (I worried for a while, actually, that this was due to wearing too-small shoes as a teenager.) As I long ago gave up stuffing them into ill-fitting high heels, except on very odd occasions, they don't twist in horrible ways, suffer from more than the odd blister or generally cause me to hide them away in the summer.

But, and it is a considerable but, if I wore half the shoes I wanted to they wouldn't look or feel this good at all. So I have settled on soft leather loafers or simple pumps for summer, always with some kind of inner-sole support as I suffer from pavement-pounding pain in the heels. In winter I wear similarly round or square-toed leather boots or shoes or, I confess, trainers – of a stylish kind I hope. (Needless to say both Uggs and Birkenstocks feature in my wardrobe, despite my slight doubt about their style credibility.)

Black satin, high-heeled Manolo Blahnik pumps or one of my two pairs of couture-made Jimmy Choos (ok, one pair for my wedding so not exactly re-usable) are the only moderately bearable shoes I own for smart evenings out. I would rather not think about those pairs of strappy heels in cream or purple,

Shoes are made by moulding the fabric of the shoe around a shoe last, traditionally made from wood but nowadays more often made from plastic.

Mass-produced shoes are made around different lasts for each style of shoe; one for a sandal, a different one for a boot. In this way manufacturers can vary not only the style of the shoe but the toe shape, heel height and so on. Each pair of shoes made on the same last will be identical.

Custom-made shoes are cast from a last of an individual's foot measurements, enabling a shoe to fit perfectly. No single person's foot is the same as another's, nor is your left foot the same as your right – it is common for variations to reach up to half a shoe size.

The process of custom-making shoes is long (typically around three months for the first pair) and far more expensive than even the best-quality mass-produced shoes. A first pair can cost up to £1,500, with a slight reduction for subsequent orders as the last is already made. But the durability of such shoes is often greater than that of other shoes, the comfort and benefits for foot problems is unsurpassed, and most bespoke shoe-makers will offer a full repair service. The best firms will offer advice on specific foot problems, fit shoes with insoles and add individual flourishes to ensure a truly unique pair of shoes.

those too-small pointed flats or all the other mistakes relegated to the shoe desert at the back of my wardrobe. There are a few more dynamic exceptions, woven platform sandals (fine if I'm going in the car) or plush purple evening slippers that are occasionally dragged out, but I pretty much live in the same four or five pairs.

Reading this back, four or five pairs as my stalwart shoe wardrobe sounds on the one hand measly but on the other rather extravagant. I won't even hazard a guess as to how many pairs I own – maybe somewhere around 40 . . . maybe 50 if you count all those cheap white pumps? (I can hear my husband snorting in disbelief in the background.) But I am honestly no Imelda Marcos, despite my love of beautiful shoes, and there are plenty of women out there to whom this number is a drop in the ocean.

Things a Woman Should Know About Shoes

But, getting back to choosing the right shoes for your feet, it all comes down to a combination of comfort, your personal style and budget. Though the concept of a capsule wardrobe seems horribly 1980s there is something to be said for a shoe cull, keeping only what you really need . . . and can fit into.

Capsule wardrobe

First of all you need to know what kind of shoes suit your feet. This is pretty much common sense, but in a nutshell:

Small, wide feet need small, wide shoes. Trainers are obviously fine but, more stylishly, so are leather shoes with wide round or square toes, and the various boat-like, very-wide-toed hippy shoes are perfect. You are unlucky if you like the look of narrow pumps because your feet will rebel if you try and stuff them in.

Podiatrists tend to recommend lace-ups rather than slip-ons for obvious support reasons. Small feet suffer in heels because the weight of the wearer is thrown closer to the ball of the foot than in women with larger feet, making balance more difficult and injury more likely. If you are short it comes as a blow that you are better off in lower heels.

Teeny-tiny feet are difficult to find shoes for if you are an adult. Of course you can shop in children's stores, which should give you a very well-fitting shoe, children's designs being that much more focused on fit, although adult feet are very different from a child's chubby paws. And style-wise you could suffer. Ballet pumps might be a good option – they look daintily appropriate on petite women and since a surge in popularity they are available in more than baby-doll pink for small feet. Take heart that these day all manner of adult shoes, from loafers to sandals, are produced in mini-me children's sizes if you get desperate.

Long, narrow feet are in many ways a dream but in fact most shoes these days are relatively wide, particularly in larger sizes, and it is hard to solve the problem of baggy gaps at the edge of your shoes as insoles don't really work for this. That aside, you can wear pointed-toe shoes more easily although these are never recommended for long-term wearing. Elegant sandals with few straps make the most of showing off your shape, and heel-wearing should come easily.

Big, long, wide feet – oh dear, the worst of all worlds will limit your shoe options, but take heart that when you do find a pair that fits they will probably fit well so your feet should be in good shape. Styles like baggy sheepskin boots are tempting but offer little support (not to mention how overpowering they are in big sizes) but the more orthopaedic styles of shoe (not untrendy these days) to true support shoes come in a good range of sizes and will fit well. Those with low or flat arches should follow the same advice and get supportive moulded soles.

Once you have sorted out what kinds of shoes are good for your feet, the harder question is reconciling this with your lifestyle. But, assuming you lead a relatively normal life with a degree of walking and carrying of shopping, a need for smartness sometimes, casual at others, with nights out a rare but worth-dressing-up-for occasion, the following should accommodate:

Flats: daytime, comfortable shoes for summer and winter. Fashion notwithstanding, what you *need* rather than want is a trusty classic shoe – loafer, ballet pump, lace-up brogue all suffice, depending on season and your own style. Ideally you should own a pair of shoes for every day of the week (!) so that your shoes can be rotated. Every day might sound extreme but two or three pairs are essential for foot health. Wearing the same pair day in, day out leads to bacterial build-up and your foot moulding unhealthily to the same shape.

Heels: a low-heeled shoe or boot is good for daytime and a higher heel is a wardrobe essential for certain occasions. I would always pick a stiletto heel as the most stylish, until you reach an age when it looks tarty or your feet simply won't oblige. Only you will know when this is! Otherwise the lower kitten heel or a low, Jackie Kennedy-style block heel are good options.

Trainers: unfortunately (or fortunately) for most women these are wardrobe staples. Judgement is essential in picking appropriate designs for the right uses: high-tech sports for the gym, simple sneakers for summer, discreet-designer for feeling stylish and comfortable at the same time.

Sandals: even if just for holiday these are hard to do without. Go glamorous and expensive if you can justify it but a couple of pairs of flip-flops, disposed of at the end of summer, will suffice, and your feet shouldn't suffer as the wear is limited. Strappy sandals only if you are *sure* you can carry it off . . . are you an A-list celebrity with a pedicure budget to match?

Boots: ankle boots are the winter equivalent of flat shoes. Knee-high versions are indispensable in winter beneath skirts and over jeans or even (this may be a terrible fashion faux pas by next year) leggings.

So, those other 33 never-worn pairs in your wardrobe: Ebay, friends, charity . . . in that order.

The Insiders

There are many women for whom shopping for shoes is an experience they can never get enough of – the fantasy, the promise of the shoe that will transform her from suburban housewife to midnight vamp . . . well, maybe not quite, but shoe shopping *is* an indulgence for many of us.

The same, unfortunately, cannot be said of shopping for socks. Tights have become interesting on a fashion level of late and stockings are a whole different kind of thrilling (so I am told) but your boring shoe-lining sock is more likely to be something you pick up with the groceries at the Marks & Spencer checkout.

Without them, however, our feet would be in trouble: sweaty and blistered in summer, cold, damp and prone to infection in winter. Our shoes would fill with bacteria, smell and then rot; our feet would be shedding skin faster than a snake and be riddled with warts and verrucae. A sorry picture and a little melodramatic but it illustrates the purpose of socks nicely. After all, we have been wearing socks of a sort since Ancient times: the word comes from the Latin *soccus*, a kind of loose, low-heeled slipper that the Greeks wore inside sandals and as slippers around the home. There are some shoes that can be worn without socks, but most need them for all of the above reasons.

Once you start to look, there is a whole new world of socks out there and it is strangely compelling. Try the ultimate indulgence: throwing out your entire sock drawer and replenishing it with socks that have no holes, have elastic that stays up and, best of all, match!

Why is it that you can own ten pairs of identical socks but when it comes to pairing them somehow they never seem to match? Oh and of course that inevitable singleton whose mate has gone to the place no one knows, where socks disappear to (and pens).

A friend of mine once said that if she became incredibly rich she would wear a brand new pair of socks every day and I can see her point. There is something about pulling on an unwrinkled, fine dark sock that makes feet look perfect and your best shoes rather shabby.

Things a Woman Should Know About Shoes

Dark socks are the norm as we tend to wear dark shoes. Choose cotton with no more than 5 percent of man-made stretch in them. The silky viscose ones look great with formal clothes but make your feet sweat.

Don't just wear black! Wear brown, navy, grey, and red if you dare. No one will know until you casually cross your legs on the tube. A minor dare but as gratifying as wearing absurdly expensive underwear under a boring work suit.

Knee-high socks make me think first of school and next of all those super-trendy Japanese girls in their mock-kindergarten short skirts, socks and pigtails, Hello Kitty bags flying. My son simply associates knee socks with football players.

Ankle socks should somehow be spelled 'sox'. I am not a fan although they are useful in trainers during summer when it is impossible to go barefoot. I have been known to approximate a pair by borrowing my three-year-old's – a top tip for mothers who run out!

Summer brings out those singularly unattractive 'American Tan' nylon 'foot-liners' that look like catering hair-nets for the feet. What's more they inevitably tear, don't stop your feet smelling, and poke out from all shoes unattractively despite their supposed invisibility.

Things a Woman Should Know About Shoes

The longer cousins of these foot-nets are, of course, pop-socks. I really have nothing against pop-socks, after all a more hygienic alternative to yeast-promoting tights under trousers and far less troublesome than stockings, but only if you can't see them. There is no excuse for wearing them with long (or worse, short) skirts where every move of your leg reveals a swollen, elastic-encircled chunk of calf. This makes the recent trend for schoolgirls to wear pop-socks with their beaten-up ballet flats, coupled with a good couple of inches of displayed flesh before the school skirt is reached, all the more mysterious.

Ankle versions of opaque tights are a clever invention, although still less breathable than cotton socks, and they cling so tightly that they leave dreadful sock marks. (Tight elastic is a serious problem for anyone with diabetes or high blood pressure, or during pregnancy, when blood clots are a risk.)

Longer still are stockings, in theory healthy and stylish or even glamorous (read sexy) in a clichéd way. But stockings mean suspender belts, so for most of us you can forget it. Hold-ups are the industry's answer to the problem but the fetish rubber band that grips your thigh so tightly in order that they stay up has always put me off. This band is also very tight and not necessarily healthy – see above.

Tights are a winter staple but can be itchy, sweaty and fall down. The newer crop of thick cotton or cotton/wool are more successful. If wearing nylons that feel unbearably tight on the stomach (tummy ache and terrible wind common side-effects), simply cut the gusset. Seems wasteful but it works.

Tights come in patterns that can be seen as a fashion statement – even fishnets have been deemed stylish. But patterned socks are riskier. Argyll, beloved of golfers, is classic though not necessarily fashionable – think pink and yellow worn under pale jeans in Chelsea boots. Striped socks I like, but spotty socks are a gimmick too far.

There are socks for all occasions, my favourite of which must be bed-socks. Despite the fact that your feet get too hot after the first ten minutes there is nothing as lovely as padding around in a dressing gown and socks (preferably cashmere . . . the gown too). Beware of the rugged wool versions. Though pleasingly textured and comfortable-looking to the eye they itch like crazy.

Socks in winter are a given but should we forgo them in summer? No, say the experts. It is even more important to wear a cotton lining in the bug-promoting heat of summer.

Things a Woman Should Know About Shoes

I agree that in trainers and any shoe where you don't see the sock this is good advice. But there are some shoes that can't be worn with socks if you are wearing a skirt, dress or pair of cropped trousers. Unless you want to look really silly.

In this case I would advise wearing good leather shoes (as breathable as cotton socks), not wearing them every day, and keeping an eye on foot hygiene. There are a number of anti-fungal or anti-bacterial sprays that will freshen up shoes and feet if you can bear the smell (or the thought of all those chemicals on your skin).

All in all socks are under-estimated. We may be used to wearing the same old holey pairs year in, year out but give your sock drawer a facelift. Chuck the whole lot out and start again. And be grateful for all those extra pairs at Christmas.

Make Do and Mend

There was a time when a pair of shoes would last a lifetime – or at least a good 20 years or so. You invested, you cared and you mended.

Today, with our mentality of buy cheap and buy often, shoes are replaced as readily as any other consumer item: wear them, abuse them, then chuck them out.

But there is something to be said for looking after shoes. They look better, last longer and, best of all, you can justify spending more on them in the first place.

The pinnacle of investment shoe-buying comes in the bespoke market, more often for men than women, where shoes cost upwards of £1,500 and at that price it would be criminal not to look after them. Bespoke shoe-makers expect these pairs to last decades, not months, and will happily replace soles and heels, patch up minor damage and generally keep the shoe looking new and healthy for a long period of time. A happy side-effect is your feet stay healthy too.

As for a healthy bank balance, it does take a lot of wear to justify that kind of expenditure but a good, solid £200 pair of shoes that fit well, have a certain longevity of style about them and are well looked after can be a sensible purchase (honestly!).

I admit, this slightly smacks of that feminine logic that allows us to spend hundreds on an item in the sale because it is half price: 'It didn't *cost* me £200, it *saved* me £200 – it used to retail at £400 you know!'

But I am a great believer in cost per wear. If you buy a pair of shoes for £200 and wear them 200 times (easily done in a couple of years) it costs you a pound a wear. (This is actually a very conservative estimate. I have had good pairs of shoes that have had 500-plus wears before giving out.) If you buy a £15-pound pair of gold flip-flops and chuck them away after your holiday, same cost per wear!

It is the same with a cheap but poorly made pair of heels where the fake-satin fabric tears, the heel falls off and the few wears you do get out of them are painful and ugly as your feet bulge at the front and blister at the back.

The problem is few of us know how to care for our shoes. Here are some tips:

You should never wear the same pair of shoes twice in a row. We have more than 250,000 sweat glands on our feet and when this is trapped in shoes bacteria have a field day. Giving shoes a day or two to recover and dry out is sensible.

You may notice that shoes stored in even slightly damp conditions that are not worn frequently start to develop a green fuzz of mould. This is yet another bacterial problem and if you are being truly virtuous wipe down your shoes and store them in a dry, cool environment. There are various anti-bacterial sprays on the market for bad cases.

Shoes should be kept in shape with shoe-trees, preferably made from cedar wood, a kind of natural air freshener which will also absorb a degree of moisture. These are not cheap but worth the investment. Of course purists who demand wooden hangers for their clothes will be willing to pay for the aesthetic appeal of cedar shoe-trees. Cedar socks, a tube that can be slipped into shoes or boots, have a similarly beneficial effect although they are less helpful for maintaining shoe shape. Boots need even more help maintaining their shape so invest in some boot-trees – wooden if you can afford or find them.

Polishing leather shoes is essential to maintain condition. Use decent polish and apply with a soft cloth (old pyjamas and t-shirts are great!). Brush off with a bristle brush and finally polish with a second clean, soft cloth for maximum shine and preservation of the leather. Natural polish is the best option if you can't match a shoe colour exactly (don't try and fudge this; the wrong colour used on good shoes will mean weeks of re-polishing to restore them).

Suede should be sprayed with a specialist protector before wearing – this should really be done every couple of months – and a suede brush can be used to buff and remove stains. If the colour fades badly there are suede shampoos available.

Fabric should be similarly protected by an all-weather guard spray. In fact even leather benefits from this kind of all-purpose protection, and not just shoes: treat your handbags as well.

Things a Woman Should Know About Shoes

A load of cobblers

Mending shoes before it is too late is as important as caring for them in the first place, and all repairs should be done by a reputable cobbler.

Heels should not be left to wear down to a stump before being replaced. Leather soles may be attractive (and have style cachet) but are not hugely practical. Many shoe-makers now offer a rubber addition to leather-soled shoes or this is easily done by a shoe-mender. Rubber is weatherproof and will wear for far longer than leather. It is also not lethally slippery. If you do plan to wear new leather-soled shoes outside, scoring the soles with a knife will save many a slip-up even if it seems a terrible crime to do so. If you do stick with leather remember it wears down quite quickly and may need replacing.

Holes in shoes any other place than the sole are fairly terminal, but if it is a pair you absolutely love, a good cobbler should be able to stitch a hole, or a matching piece of leather can be inserted from the inside. The effect is not perfect but better than chucking them out in the short term.

If you have never investigated mending shoes before it is amazing what can be salvaged by a trained professional. And the longer your shoes last the less guilty you will feel about how much they cost.

The Promised Land

'Sex and the City changed New York. New York's become a big shoe store now.'

Chris Noth

Boutique designer-shoe buying has never been so popular. But can finding the perfect pair of shoes be the road to Nirvana? And if it is, can you afford it?

Despite the vast cost of designer shoes, women of all walks of life seem to be happy to hand over their credit card. This is, in part, the lure of the boutique.

From Imelda Marcos and the staggering cost of her legendary collection of 1,200 pairs of shoes to Carrie Bradshaw, the *Sex and the City* character who in one episode estimates her shoe collection to have cost her $40,000, women's total shoe spend can be colossal.

But how much are you willing to pay for a single pair of shoes? These days spending four or five hundred pounds on a single pair of shoes is par for the course. With the mounting cost of materials – in particular exotic animal skins and semi-precious jewels – it is not uncommon to find shoes costing well over £1,000. And boots are even more expensive. Be it urban myth or urban fantasy, apparently Manolo Blahnik's alligator-skin boots will set you back around £7,000.

There is an element of cost involved in design and craftsmanship too. Roger Vivier, for example, is known for his trademark curved heel but it is some feat of engineering to craft this to the sole of a shoe. And top design talent is priceless.

The ultimate Cinderella's slipper, however, appeared a couple of years ago courtesy of Stuart Weitzman, whose four-and-a-half-inch stiletto sandals were studded with diamonds equalling 55 carats, including a single five-carat stone. The price? A cool two million dollars. Dream on, the rest of us.

Walking into any chi-chi designer boutique is intimidating but in a thrilling kind of way. When I was at university my best friend and I used to dare ourselves to brave the bodyguards and enter the hallowed sanctums of the designer stores on Sloane Street and Bond Street. Once in, a lipstick or a key-chain gave us a taste of the dream.

This is precisely the appeal of shoes. They are a way of buying into an otherwise impossible dream, particularly if you are not in possession of a celebrity body size. Dresses may be out of your reach but shoes are not. Money-wise, too, a pair of shoes may be very expensive for what they are but far cheaper than a suit or even a car, let alone a house in a pricey neighbourhood.

And there is that ugly-sister fantasy that you will slip into the glass slipper and find it fits perfectly, your Prince Charming waiting to spirit you away.

Alas, none of this is any more than an expensive daydream, but women the world over still keep on buying it.

But, shopping-savvy as we have become, it is increasingly common to buy any designer garment, shoes or otherwise, at a discount price, through the mainstream sales, outlet shopping or even on Ebay (where, I am told, shoes can be bought for a pittance). For some the buzz comes from the hushed atmosphere of the boutique, the attention of the sales assistants and the glossy carrier bag. No such high once you get home, unfortunately, more like a guilty low.

For most of us the buzz is far greater to find a £300 pair of shoes for £50. Badly addicted shoe-aholics take note.

When all else fails simply remove yourself from temptation. As actress Katie Holmes put it:

'It's actually great to shoot far away from Hollywood because we don't have the distraction of the parties and premieres and all that. And, of course, you can save money — there are no good shoe stores.'

A Work of Art

Shoes may be the holy grail of fashionistas and celebrities but with their sculptural qualities and symbolic message they have also been a source of inspiration for some of the most famous artists of the twentieth century.

Shoes may be prominently featured within works of art but they are also commonly exhibited as works of art in their own right. There are an extraordinary number of shoe museums around the world. The Bata Shoe Museum in Toronto, Canada, for example, houses over 10,000 shoes.

Take Van Gogh's boots, for example: in an essay by German philosopher Heidegger, no fewer than eight paintings of workers' boots by the painter are interpreted as representing the nobility of the peasant woman. The boots are a symbol of the true essence of the worker. In fact, these boots have been widely interpreted as not belonging to a peasant at all but to the painter himself. It brings to mind the few times I have come across esteemed artist Lucien Freud, also habitually dressed in paint-splattered worker boots – even in the smartest restaurants.

The Surrealist sculptures of the 1920s and 1930s included shoes and other types of footwear in their works created from everyday objects; feminist artists claimed the high heel to be a symbol of women's oppression. There is no doubt that a pair of spike-heeled pumps, in contrast to earthy workers' boots, would be universally agreed to represent sexuality and womanliness, perhaps even with a hint of danger or sin. It is no wonder that erotica and pornography frequently feature shoes of this kind.

Salvador Dali also favoured the disembodied shoe, featuring pumps, espadrilles and brogues among his works both sculptural and painted. And more recently, photographers of all kinds have seized on the sculptural possibilities of the shoe to create striking images, not least in the world of fashion photography.

Things a Woman Should Know About Shoes

Smaller shoe exhibitions are set up in museums such as London's Victoria and Albert, and it is gratifying to hear that the famous shoe-lover Imelda Marcos set up the Markina City Shoe Museum in Manila, hoping to put many of her extensive collection to good use and, as she explained, crown the Philippines the shoe capital of the world. It makes the idea of putting unworn, ill-fitting but horribly expensive shoes bought in haste or passion into a display cabinet not such a bad one after all.

Last but not least, film-makers have used shoes to various effects. Several versions have been made of the classic Hans Christian Andersen fairy tale *The Red Shoes*, but even when shoes are not the primary subject matter of a film there are plenty of ways in which they are used symbolically when portraying a character. Film costume designers have a field day when it comes to dressing characters, with many a classic movie moment zooming in on a pair of stiletto-clad legs disappearing into the distance.

Be Kind to Your Daughter

Shopping for children's shoes is a whole different ball game. Style goes out of the window in favour of fit. Or at least that is how small girls (and perhaps boys) perceive it.

My best and worst shoe memories from childhood are as follows. Best: a simple pair of gold mules I either bought or stole from my mother (I vaguely recollect teetering around in a pair far too big, so perhaps the latter) aged around five or six. I wore them with dresses, shorts, my nightie . . . anything. Heaven.

My worst memory was later, in early adolescence, maybe aged 12 or so. The parties I was being invited to had begun to involve boys, though, as is true today, I was more concerned about the consensus of my female peers. This particular party

was during high summer and, incredibly, my outfit managed to satisfy both my mother and my hyper-critical self, puppy-fat and all.

The shoes, however, were the sticking point. My mother (probably quite rightly) refused to buy me a wholly inappropriate pair of possibly slutty shoes, saying my solid Clarks sandals were fine. They were technically fine, I suppose, but as far as street-cred went, disastrous. Flat, wide, navy blue and buckled. I will remember the humiliation to this day. Of course half the other girls were wearing similar and praying it was an outdoor event with long grass. Oh, the agony of childhood.

So, be kind to your daughters and respect that form is almost as important as function, even when you are three years old.

Advice for mothers: *do* make fit a priority; there is no excuse for ruining your children's feet. Have them measured by a professional and bear in mind that small children's feet can go up a size in as little as eight weeks.

Accept that small girls like pink, glitter and anything that makes them resemble a princess, fairy or ballerina. Small boys (in my limited experience) actually care just as much (boots make them a policeman, light-up trainers a superhero, etc.) so try offering a choice of two pairs and let them decide. A parental-trickery sense that they control their environment works wonders when getting dressed in the morning. ('Look! You can wear the shoes *you* chose.') And if your boy wants to wear beaten-up boots and socks with shorts rather than sandals, let him. It looks rather charming in a scruffy-urchin kind of way.

Buy cheap wellies. Children look cute in all Wellington boots and they grow out of them so quickly, despite the appeal of all those animal-head affairs. Leave those for doting grandparents to indulge in.

Luckily there are many more styles around than when we were children, although school shoes are still that same leaden shape and look dreadful and beaten up within days of first wearing (are children really so bad?). Although I suppose it is better they fit in than wear something that gets them beaten up in the playground. (Apparently designer-trainer wars have reached such highs in some schools that trainers are banned altogether. Not a bad idea if your little darling has come home wearing only socks and a tearful expression.)

Lastly, *don't* pass shoes down to younger siblings – they are the only wearable items that should be exclusive to one child (though second-hand undies are a bit harsh). And *do* put shoes together in pairs somewhere you can find them to avoid stress-induced headaches prior to the school run each day.

Golden Rules

In this book I have tried to cover as much as possible about wearing, choosing, buying and caring for shoes. There are so many different types of footwear that it is almost impossible to summarize the essentials of a successful (and loving) relationship with your shoe collection . . . and hopefully to look good at the same time.

There are, however, some golden rules that are worth bearing mind and, should you feel so inclined, ignoring on occasion. After all, shoes are a very personal thing – even more than clothes, a well-chosen pair of shoes is a way of pulling a look together or expressing our flamboyant side. And what else can fit in your handbag and allow you to change an outfit completely before stepping out of the office and on to the town?

But with the choice of shoes, both designer and high-street, growing all the time, it is helpful to have a few guidelines that might rein in shoe spending a little bit. So here they are – the rules that will stand everyone from the shoe virgin to the shoe vixen in good stead:

Unless you have money to burn, consider your lifestyle before buying any pair of shoes. There is nothing more depressing than owning beautiful pairs of shoes you never have occasion to wear – worst-case scenario call your Choos a work of art and put them on display in your boudoir.

Actually, there is one thing more depressing than owning shoes you have no occasion to wear, and that is owning beautiful shoes that don't fit. Probably the most important rule of all is BUY SHOES THAT FIT!

For your best chance of getting a good-fitting shoe, look at your feet – are they long and narrow, short and stumpy, already suffering from bunions and corns? Use your common sense and don't even bother trying on shoes you know will squash, hurt or otherwise mutilate your precious feet. Then try on the pair you think might fit. Try on the size below and the size above. Try on in the morning and after a hot day pounding the pavement. Be sure. Particularly if you are spending a lot of money.

Things a Woman Should Know About Shoes

Remember high heels change not only your posture but your attitude. Great for confidence and sex appeal. Learn to walk in stilettos but be discriminating about when you wear them. And take full advantage of those cushion-pads and heel-grips designed for hard-to-wear shoes.

Designer shoes may be seductive but see through the label and packaging. You are probably not an A-list celebrity with a budget to match. That said, an expensive pair of shoes that *look* expensive make a not-so-pricey outfit look like a million dollars.

Boots are as essential as shoes to a woman's wardrobe. But they cost a lot more and are only good in winter, so choose carefully.

Trainers are comfortable, useful and practical but essentially un-stylish. Try hard to find a moderately good-looking pair if they are to be your wardrobe staple. Expectant mothers, don't ignore this advice – they *will* become your favourite thing to wear buggy-pushing.

Sandals are often uncomfortable, no good for walking long distances and require you to buff and polish your feet, but summer wouldn't be the same without them. Sandals aside, the best thing about summer is the chance to walk barefoot on the beach – good for body and soul (sole!).

Things a Woman Should Know About Shoes

Shoes only look as good as the feet that wear them, but the state (and good looks) of your feet is determined by the shoes you choose. A love–hate relationship if ever there was one. Badly shod feet will rebel, causing painful lumps and bumps that in turn ruin the shape of the shoes you try to wear. Mutual respect and looking after both shoes and feet is the answer.

Have pedicures and chiropody; tend to blisters, bunions and corns sooner rather than later. Carry plasters, wear socks when you can and vary the shoes you wear – your feet will thank you.

Buy some shoe polish, invest in some shoe-trees and make friends with your local shoe-mender. Resist the disposable-world mentality, look after what you have got and make do and mend.

Don't wear the same pair of shoes day in, day out. They will smell, lose their shape and affect the health of your feet.

Your feet, like the rest of your body, change as you get older. Weight gain, pavement pounding and the simple passing of the years make feet increase in length and width – a full size increase after the age of 40 is not unusual. So accept you may never wear those treasured first Manolo Blahniks again.

Three things to remember when shoe-aholism threatens to get out of hand: essentially shoes are just there to protect your feet; there are a limited number of pairs of shoes that you will actually get round to wearing before they go out of fashion; and I don't want to devalue the currency, but most people don't even notice what you are wearing on your feet.

Last but by no means least, have fun! There are so many different styles of shoe out there, both classically stylish and weird and wonderful. Fashion has claimed footwear for its own so make the most of it and don't buy the same old boring style year after year.

Conclusion

I wrote in the introduction to this book that women love shoes. Writing it has made me realize the situation is far more serious than that. Attempt a psychological analysis if you will but the bottom line, as many a cynical man (or bitter husband) has pointed out, is that women simply have a 'shoe thing' going on. (Men, be careful what accusations you make, there are plenty of boy-toy addicts out there with just as much of a problem.)

What you choose to put on your feet can transform you in so many different ways: not only the appearance of an outfit, but posture and body shape and, without sounding too evangelical, your state of mind, confidence and emotions.

Conclusion

I hope that reading this book – from cover to cover or more likely dipping a well-shod toe in here and there – has been informative and interesting, serious in parts but light-hearted too; just as a woman's relationship with shoes should be.

As I touched upon in the chapter on shoes as works of art, it is nice to remember that shoes carry not only a practical message but a metaphorical one too. There are many turns of phrase that include references to shoes or feet and as well as appearing in works of art, shoes are mentioned throughout history, in literature and in proverbs; all too often their meaning is more than literal.

Here is a selection of quotations that illustrate the point. Remember a few as ammunition against those who belittle the importance of shoes. Try hard enough and maybe you can convince yourself that your shoe obsession is far from trivial – it is, in fact, an exercise in philosophy.

'The shoe that fits one person pinches another; there is no recipe for living that fits all cases.'

Carl Jung

Things a Woman Should Know About Shoes

'A shoe that is too large is apt to trip one, and when too small to pinch the feet. So it is with those whose fortune does not suit them.'

Horace

'The wearer knows best where the shoe pinches.'

Irish Proverb

'Who will wear a shoe that hurts him, because the shoe-maker tells him 'tis well made?'

Algernon Sydney

'What spirit is so empty and blind, that it cannot recognize the fact that the foot is more noble than the shoe, and skin more beautiful than the garment with which it is clothed?'

Michelangelo

'If the shoe fits, wear it.'

Proverb

Conclusion

'If the shoe fits, it is probably worn out.'

Craig Bruce

'If the shoe fits, it's too expensive!'

Adrienne Gusoff

'Now for good luck, cast an old shoe after me.'

Proverb

Things a Woman Should Know About Shoes

The publishers would like to thank the following sources for their kind permission to reproduce the pictures in this book:

Alamy Images: /Martin Carlsson: page 40; /ClassicStock: page 180; /John Robertson: page 93; /Steve Sant: page 36; /Vario Images GmbH & Co. KG: pages 76–7

The Bridgeman Art Library/Fogg Art Museum: page 176

Corbis Images: /Bettmann: page 197; /Julio Donoso/SYGMA: page 133; /Tim Graham: pages 148–9; /Hulton-Deutsch Collection: pages 28–9; /G. June/zefa: page 109; /Gail Mooney: page 49; /Donald Nausbaum: page 89; /William Perlman/Star Ledger: page 157; /Dario Pignatelli/Reuters: page 32; /Steve Sands/New York Newswire: page 140; /Mark Savage: page 121; /Stapleton Collection: page 12; /Sunset Boulevard/SYGMA: page 189; /Adrianna Williams/zefa: pages 184–5

Getty Images: /Altrendo Images: page 125; /Bridgeman Art Library: page 16; /China Photos: page 128; /Jeffrey Coolidge/Iconica: page 5; /Amanda Edwards: page 45; /Alfred Eisenstaedt/Time & Life Pictures: page 96; /Fox Photos: page 196; /John Franks: page 112; /Frazer Harrison: page 44; /Dave Hogan: page 205; /Keystone Features: page 204; /Jon Kopaloff/FilmMagic: page 52; /Pascal Le Segretain: page 53;